POLITICAL STICKY WICKET:

THE UNTOUCHABLE PONZI SCHEME

OF ALLEN STANFORD

CHIDEM KURDAS

TABLE OF CONTENTS

Introduction

In February 2009, about two months after Bernard Madoff hit the news, another major financial scandal surfaced. At first glance, the two events appeared to have much in common. Robert Allen Stanford, like Madoff, defrauded numerous people for many years. Since the total amount he collected was less, Stanford came to be called a mini-Madoff or the Texas Madoff.

Both men were snared in the 2008-2009 financial crisis, which made all Ponzi schemes hard to sustain as people pulled out their money. Against this common background, the two long-time perpetrators took strikingly different tacks. Madoff, who was in no danger of being caught but recognized the near impossibility of continuing the game, went to the authorities of his own volition and confessed. He admitted the crime, took all the responsibility, pleaded guilty and went to prison without a fight.

Stanford, by contrast, already faced a threatening investigation before the crisis came to a head. But he would not give up. To the end, he tried to raise capital to compensate for losses and took aggressive steps to protect himself. Once charged, he did what he could to prevent or delay the trial; once convicted, he contested the sentence. He never confessed, never admitted a thing. He blamed everybody but himself. By all evidence he would have continued his scheme had the United States not come after him.

And why wouldn't he? For years he had defied regulators and built a financial empire around a novel conning method. He had done it all under the noses of authorities who long suspected him of laundering drug money and defrauding his clients. People in various arms of the US government knew about Stanford and were leery of him for two decades.

This book tells the story of how the bold trickster stayed one step ahead of the law and kept his scheme going against the odds. My aim is to connect the many pieces so as to reveal the broader significance of the tale.

In most swindles, including Madoff's, the key question is how the victims were lured and deceived. You study the perpetrator's dealings with his marks. But in the case of Stanford, another set of relationships were pivotal — his connections to government entities and officials.

To protect his racket, he cultivated a web of wide-ranging alliances with financial regulators, politicians and possibly law enforcement agencies. Those extensive contacts allowed his empire to spread across the globe and to continue operating as he fought off repeated attempts to expose his charade.

Officially, fraud is something that happens in markets; the role of the government is to fight it. This is one of the core responsibilities of a state, part of its law and order mandate. People of all political stripes expect the public realm to perform such basic functions — in return for taxes collected and limits on freedom imposed in the name of the common good. How fraud is battled bears on the question of how well a government holds its end of the bargain with citizens.

Less acknowledged is that government entities themselves enable fraud. Some of the best known financial shenanigans in history happened under public auspices. Markets alone could never have generated these gigantic crony schemes.

Thus the 18th century "Mississippi" bubble in France had behind it the ruler of that country at the time, the Regent.[1] The idea came from the notorious gambler and paper money advocate John Law, but it was only after he got the Regent's backing that he was able to put it into effect. The bank that Law founded to issue notes was under royal decree and became a public institution — in effect, a central bank. Similarly, the South Sea bubble in England started as an effort to finance government debt and the South Sea Company gave a kind of stock option to selected members of the government and their associates.[2]

While I could give other examples, those two are enough to demonstrate that crony schemes have a long and lurid pedigree; Stanford is by no means unique. But he is a remarkable specimen of the modern well-connected fraudster with global reach. Government interplay with financial fraud takes diverse forms in modern societies. He mastered the modes of operation in different places and played them all. What makes him especially intriguing is his success in the complex political environment of the United States.

There is no better evidence of this than a photograph published in the *Antigua Sun*, one of the two Caribbean newspapers Stanford owned. Dated June 2008, the picture shows two men in dark suits posing together, both smiling to reveal a wide expanse of teeth. The caption identifies one as Sir Allen Stanford and the other as Senator Barack Obama, who of course is instantly recognizable. The accompanying text says they met in Miami where the presidential candidate gave a speech.[3]

The then-Senator was one of hundreds of politicians from both parties to whom Stanford contributed and with whom he had himself photographed. This particular image is striking nevertheless. It shows that the long-running contest of Allen Stanford versus justice is not just a matter for investors and financial sleuths. His encounters with Congressmen and Senators, Presidents and Prime Ministers and other high-level officials, are of interest to anyone who wants to understand how governments put into practice their supposed mission of preventing fraud.

There is a great deal of printed, broadcast and web-posted information about Stanford, his past and his business, some of it wrong and large portions of it questionable. I have based my account on legal documents where possible and when using news sources and interviews, compared the evidence to identify inconsistencies. When reports diverge significantly from the known or the plausible, I've pointed out the conflict. The sources are listed at the end of the book and key references are given in endnotes.

Stanford and his advocates claimed that he was railroaded by government officials who made a scapegoat of him so as to ward off criticism of the Madoff fiasco. This suggests that the official record contains falsehoods.

Certainly the Madoff debacle forced regulators' hand and made them act with greater dispatch. But the real question is not why they nabbed Stanford; rather, it is why they did not do so much earlier.

Having gone through reams of material, including the immense paperwork generated by the many lawsuits that he left in his wake, I am convinced that legal documents are as reliable a source of information as one can get on this matter. That does not mean information is available about all of his adventures.

There are many things we do not know about Stanford, in particular his relationships with certain parts of the United States government. Investigations and decisions by the Securities and Exchange Commission are reasonably well documented but not those by other agencies. Similarly, his activities in certain countries are better known than in others. His doings in Antigua are notorious, but he operated in many countries and may have played a less recognized role in some.

I make no claim to have the complete set of facts, only enough to establish the main storyline, which is extraordinary as it is. What we know is sufficient to delineate an audacious scoundrel who merged, to an exceptional degree, financial fraud with political corruption.

Could he be innocent, as he asserted? While some aspects of his long escapade may appear in a different light if significant new facts emerge, I find it impossible to imagine the central theme changing.

Stanford was a greater crook than most others in recent decades; that would be hard to refute. His innovative ploy for deceiving people, pitiless pursuit of helpless victims and use of political influence made him a distinctive schemer on a grand scale, far removed from garden variety hucksters.

His machinations were unusually nasty, causing his victims to suffer extreme hardship. In the United States, he ripped off the life savings of retirees, some of them blue-collar workers who were reduced to poverty by the loss he inflicted. At the same time, one has to admit that he was colorful and lively, indeed one of the more flashy characters in the centuries-old history of financial schemes.

I Could Not Stay

Only a few of Stanford's claims ring true. One of these gives a sense of what he wanted in life. "I could not stay in a small town and be content," he told a reporter.[4] That's convincing, even though he expertly shaped his public image by planting suggestive tidbits and cooked-up anecdotes, using careful evasions and outright lies.

Other rogues expressed similar feelings about themselves. Thus Robert Vesco recalled that the first of his three priorities was "To get the hell out of Detroit."

For Allen Stanford, the place to escape from was Mexia in central Texas, its prosperous heyday in the 1920s oil boom long past by the time he was born in March 1950. The town was poorer than other parts of Texas, its early 20th century handsome brick buildings marred by shabby storefronts and empty spaces. And it was socially tight laced.

Stanford's great-great grandfather had settled in Mexia after the civil war. His grandfather, Lodis, was a barber who became an insurance salesman and started an insurance brokerage in 1932, in the midst of the Great Depression. Allen's father, James, inherited this business and stayed in Mexia. At one time he was the town's mayor. He appears to have been content with his life.

But Allen's mother reportedly felt constrained by the old-fashioned culture. She got a divorce when Allen was nine years old and moved to Fort Worth, taking him and his brother with her. Both she and his father remarried. The children appear to have had a comfortable enough middle-class upbringing, suffering no major hardship from the divorce of the parents.

Allen went back to Mexia regularly and kept his ties to relatives in the area. Those connections continued through his career. In his official biography, the family firm with its 70-plus-year history was front and center. His enterprising grandfather became an inspirational tale. He named a conference room after Lodis, had a documentary made about him and in interviews mentioned the insurance brokerage started in the Great Depression. His father and an old friend from Mexia sat on the board of his company.

By all accounts Allen was an enterprising and hard working youth. He pitched his old bicycle to a possible buyer and did not shirk from physically grueling labor. After some trouble settling down at a college, he ended up at Baylor University in Waco, the alma mater of his father. There he found himself a roommate named James Davis. On the side he taught scuba diving, which engaged his interest more than classes and homework.

Davis recalled, "while the rest of us were beating our brains out, he was making himself a lot of money teaching scuba diving." Stanford not only earned money but won a trip to the Caribbean for his diving prowess. Sports, the Caribbean and Davis were to be mainstays of his life.

After graduating from Baylor with a degree in business administration, he continued to demonstrate a can-do spirit. At age 25 he got married to a girl from a town near Mexia and they had a daughter. He found partners and with them took over a gym in Waco, named it Total Fitness and charged a high fee for membership.

It looks like he wanted to develop a chain of athletic clubs; he started a large one in Houston, was involved in others. He had found the right business niche – one that reflected his interest in sports – and was doing well. He bought a flashy car.

Then disaster struck. Three blows hit the Texas economy. In the early 1980s the price of oil collapsed. That undermined the local real estate boom. As developers went bust and defaulted on loans, they took down with them a number of savings and loans associations.[5] The combined oil and property slumps and S&L crisis resulted in dire economic conditions.

Stanford had over-expanded the gyms and assumed enough customers would be willing to pay the fee. He was extremely vulnerable to the downturn — gym memberships are one of the discretionary spending items people typically cut when they face job and income loss. As revenues dropped, he could not meet his obligations. By 1983, Total Fitness club was bankrupt.

Creditors sued Stanford; his former partners hounded him. There were rumors that he was arrested, but he did not go to prison. He and his wife filed for personal bankruptcy. In 1984, he was 34 and insolvent, with debts of $13.6 million against assets of less than $230,000. This had to be an infuriating result for a hard-driving man determined to run his own business and get out to the wider world.

A burger joint he started in Waco also failed. Talk of excessive drinking as well as legal tangles dented his prospects. He was in danger of having to spend the rest of his life working for his father's insurance brokerage in Mexia. Another person might have settled for that, but not Allen Stanford.

The slow pace and staid lifestyle did not appeal to him. One way or the other, he would escape. In this respect as well as others, he resembled another flamboyant adventurer who came out of Mexia, one Vickie Lynn Hogan, better known by the name she assumed as a model, Anna Nicole Smith.[6]

There are several parallels between Robert Allen and Anna Nicole, besides their desire not to stay in Mexia. They were both physically imposing — the strapping Stanford stood 6ft 4in; Smith was a statuesque blond, though later on the hefty side. Both scraped their way up, ruthless in pursuit of success. While they followed entirely different routes, the same theme dominated their steep upward climb, namely getting, fighting for and spending large sums of money.

Both went through numerous lovers. One of Stanford's early girlfriends reportedly worked for his health clubs; she took his name and they had a child. Although he remained married, mistresses and out-of wedlock children became his pattern. Both overindulged; Smith, known for boozing and pill popping, died of an overdose. Stanford's drinking problem flared up now and then, though for much of his life he kept it under control in public.

They took huge risks as they pursued the intertwined dream of escape and riches. For a long time their luck held and in their different ways they found gold. Their lives appeared fabulously privileged to the millions who saw them on television or read about them in magazines. Then they ran out of good fortune, which is unreliable and capricious, as Machiavelli remarked in his advice to the ambitious.[7]

Stanford Oaks

With the Texas economy depressed, the Houston area was full of foreclosed buildings available at drastically cut prices. Allen and his father went into property speculation. James sold the insurance brokerage, possibly at Allen's suggestion. They bought apartment buildings from owners who were already bankrupt or in financial trouble. The father-son team managed these properties until the market recovered and they could sell at a profit.

In 1988-1989 they went into development, building clusters of high-end townhouses. Allen, his wife Susan and their daughter lived in the first of these, called Stanford Oaks. Another, called Stanford Lofts, was in downtown Houston.

The initial financing for property purchases must have come from the sale of the brokerage inherited from Lodis. But that by itself can't account for the expansion into construction. The insurance brokerage was small — it quickly disappeared into another business, which in turn fast disappeared into another, leaving no trace. It could not have been worth much money, especially in a down economy.

How did Allen finance townhouse development? He said he raised funds from Latin American investors interested in Texas real estate. It is clear that he received capital from somebody. The property ventures were a turning point. He made money, learned about real estate and cultivated a network of investors. We know nothing about the latter.

Allen's next venture comes as a startling surprise. At the end of 1985 he started an offshore bank on Montserrat, a tiny Caribbean island with fewer residents than a single Manhattan block. It was called Guardian International Bank; Stanford was president and chief executive officer; his father was a partner.

In explaining how he got rich, Allen always credited the family firm and the fortune he made with his father in real estate. That wealth supposedly allowed him to get into banking, with the senior Stanford providing the capital.

But the story that they made a killing in real estate and put that into the bank is not consistent with the known timeline. Texas did not recover for years — vacancy rates were still high in the Houston area in 1990. The Montserrat bank happened too soon to be financed by the flipping of Texas real estate. To sell the properties at a large gain, the Stanfords had to wait longer.

It is questionable how large a fortune Allen and James made. Sure, the strategy of buying up cheap properties would eventually pay. But they could not have had much capital to invest and did not borrow from banks. It is very unlikely that any bank would lend to Allen knowing that he had recently gone bankrupt. Reports of his arrest and drunken behavior wouldn't help either. Besides, Texas was in a credit crunch and even perfectly respectable businessmen had trouble getting loans.

The amount of property acquired could not be substantial unless Allen got a lot of money from his Latin American contacts. In his subsequent career he exhibited a remarkable ability in this particular endeavor, but it is not clear how much his early effort raised.

Accounts regarding what the Stanfords made on the property deals vary widely, from a couple of million dollars to hundreds of millions over 10 years.[8] Allen was the source of the high-end numbers, which sound like wishful thinking.

The father continued to live modestly in Mexia, in a single-storey house the family owned since the 1920s. He gave no indication that he was worth a hundred million dollars. People who knew him did not think he was wealthy; he never claimed to be.

Neither did the son appear to be rich until much later. Likely they made a million or two and Allen looked for ways to finance more ambitious real estate projects.

The Hole

Guardian International Bank specialized in a product called certificate of deposit. CDs issued by American banks are similar to savings accounts. CDs have a fixed maturity date but like savings accounts are protected by the FDIC, the Federal agency that guarantees deposits (up to a certain amount). American banks pay into a fund for this purpose.

Given those features, US bank CDs carry very little risk. By the same token, they pay a low rate of interest. Because of that, as a rule CDs make sense only for people who are more interested in the safety of their money than the return.

Stanford's bank was not subject to American law – being offshore in Montserrat – and not covered by Federal deposit insurance. Since he did not pay into the FDIC fund and his bank was in a low-tax jurisdiction, his costs were lower that American banks'.

From the depositors' perspective, the notable thing about Guardian CDs was the interest. It was several percentage points above the rates available from American banks.

While earning higher returns, the Guardian product was pitched as extremely safe, as a CD is supposed to be. Marketing materials attributed the better return to a portfolio of investments designed for low risk. According to these brochures, reliable outside managers picked high-quality stocks and bonds that could be sold quickly when needed.

The bank started small but the CDs apparently caught on. At the end of 1987 Guardian had deposits of just a few million dollars, but in little over a year reported deposits reached about $55 million, a growth of more than twenty-fold. Around that time Stanford hired his former college roommate Davis as controller.

He told his friend the bank was offshore so as to escape US regulatory vetting and asked him not to talk with the senior Stanford without first checking with him. It would seem he knew his father would not approve of some of the things he did.

By 1990, the bank reported $100 million in deposits. Whether that was really the case is an open question, but deposits must have grown fast because in 1990 Stanford spent $50 million to buy another bank.

This explosive expansion is one of the amazing features of his career. Once the bank had substantial capital, he would be in a better position to attract customers. But how did he persuade people to buy his notes when the bank first got going?

One explanation, given by old acquaintances, was that he had exceptional charisma and energy. This was true, judging by what he was able to do. Even so, one has to wonder about the early years.

The Latin Americans who originally bought the CDs presumably knew Stanford from his real estate ventures. By one report, he set up the bank specifically for them. They invested in his property deals, invested in the CDs, then brought others along. But the bank grew fast in 1987-1988. That was too early to reap big profits from Texas property. It is hard to believe that his partners had already received large gains and were so impressed by him that they wanted to re-invest the money in his new bank.

Leaving aside the question of the timing of the Texas real estate market, that anyone would pick Stanford as their banker is surprising. He had no banking experience before he popped up in Montserrat. Why would clients trust him to run a bank when there was nothing in his past that suggested he could do such a thing?

There is no shortage of established banks to put money into; there were hundreds of offshore banks in Montserrat alone. Why would people prefer this gym operator and property speculator to bankers already in the business?

True, Stanford offered higher interest. And he did not mention the failure of his gym business or the resulting bankruptcies. Only people around Waco and Mexia knew of his past legal problems, only a few recalled occasions of drunkenness or reports that he had been arrested but avoided charges thanks to his father's help.

But even without knowing any of that, his customers had to be aware that Stanford and his CDs were untried, the startup bank an unknown. Yet they did buy the bank's notes.

Some time in the late 1980s, probably as soon as enough money was collected, Stanford diverted depositor funds into property development. Some of the real estate he put under his own name. When Davis became controller, Stanford asked him to make false entries in the general ledger, to show bogus revenues and investment portfolio balances to the Montserrat regulator.

By late 1990 at least half the bank's reported assets did not exist. In other words, there was a "hole" between what the bank owed to CD holders and the value of its portfolio. This was concealed by fake records of revenues and investment values.[9]

Stanford casually told his friend not to worry about the hole; the real estate bets were going to pay off and then there would be more than enough money to fill the gap. But in the meantime he needed more funds, so they had to quickly increase CD sales to make up for the deficiency.[10]

He looked to expand the client base. To get the word around and pitch the product, he opened offices in Houston and Miami. These venues helped sell the CDs to a wider circle of well-to-do Latin Americans who sought secure investments in the United States.

While successful in raising money, the offices in America caused legal trouble. Stanford's CD sales were not licensed, violating banking law in Texas. In 1988 and 1989 the US Office of the Comptroller of the Currency issued warnings that Stanford violated banking laws in Florida and California as well.

Around that time Montserrat, a British colony, came under pressure to tamp down on illegalities in its banks. Typically American and European governments take issue with these off-shore financial firms because of taxes. People stash their wealth in Caribbean havens to protect it from big countries' tax collectors. The source of the money is usually legal; the tax gambit may or may not be.

But British and US authorities suspected that banks in Montserrat were laundering cash from illegal sources, in particular from narcotics traffickers. Guardian International came under suspicion for taking money from the infamous Medellin and Cali drug cartels. Scotland Yard and the FBI started to investigate.

Meanwhile, the Montserrat territory's Financial Secretary scrutinized the bank from the other side, that is, to find out what it was doing with the money. Guardian was immediately found to operate "in a manner detrimental" to customers.[11] The bank did not "supply satisfactory details as to liquidity" and had a bankrupt director, that is, Stanford — who never told anyone of his bankruptcy.

Moreover, the bank had failed to submit annual financial statements and its auditor, CAS Hewlett & Co, did not qualify as an approved bank auditor. Stanford used Hewlett to hide rather than reveal financial data, to withhold "detailed information that would normally be expected in audited financial statements," according to the regulator.

Since obviously Stanford could not reveal the hole in the balance sheet and his channeling of CD funds to property ventures instead of low-risk bonds and stocks as promised, it is no surprise that he gave as little information as possible.

In view of the findings, Montserrat moved in 1990 to revoke the bank's license and force the questionable enterprise to shut down. Informed that his banking permit was about to be withdrawn, Stanford turned in the license himself. But he sued the Montserrat authority; admitted his past bankruptcy but denied the other complaints. His lawyer at the time said they won the case but Stanford decided to pull out of Montserrat anyway.

This got him out of Scotland Yard's purview.[12] The British may have wanted to get rid of him, but from the American viewpoint the result was not satisfactory. The FBI, having posted agents outside the bank to observe the comings and goings, was building evidence of drug money coming into Guardian. By shuttering the Montserrat operation, Stanford put an end to the investigation into his business on that island.

Perhaps the fracas in Montserrat made him forget to pay taxes in the United States. He and his wife were found by the Internal Revenue Service to have underreported their 1990 federal taxes by close to half a million dollars. He disputed this in US Tax Court – his typically disputed any claim against him that mattered – but lost the case.

All these experiences may have led to a determination to protect himself better next time. He had to make sure government people did not bother him; could not make him pay higher taxes, force him to reveal information or take away his license. The new location he found for his bank was just right for the purpose. And he did not have to go far.

Sticky Wicket

The islands of Antigua and Barbuda in the eastern Caribbean form a small country that ceased to be a British colony in 1981. Fine beaches and lush greenery make the twin islands natural for tourism, but 20 years ago they were undeveloped compared to other parts of the West Indies.

Antigua has attractive features—it is a stable parliamentary democracy and relatively safe, with a police force and court system based on English law.[13] Centuries of British rule left legacies like membership in the Commonwealth and the still-popular game of cricket.

The dark side was a reputation for being one of the most corrupt places in the world. The man who led the country for decades, Vere Cornwall Bird or "Papa" Bird, started as the head of the labor unions in the 1940s and founded the Antigua Labor Party. From 1951 on this party won election after election under VC Bird – except for five years in the 1970s – and in the 1990s his son, Lester Bird, took over as political leader and prime minister.

The dynasty came to be notorious, suspected of providing a refuge for drug and gun smugglers willing to pay for protection—a matter of special concern to American law enforcement agencies, given the proximity of Antigua to the US Virgin Islands and Puerto Rico.

Antigua was one of the places that sheltered the fugitive Robert Vesco as he dodged attempts to extradite him back to the United States.[14]

Most of the population remained poor despite efforts to diversify the economy away from its old mainstay, sugar production. The country was heavily in debt and the Bird governments were chronically short of money, at times unable to pay state employees' salaries. The family reportedly raided the nation's social security fund for their personal expenses.

Nor could they easily find creditors willing to lend to them, given their existing debts, poor track record and secrecy — the cabinet would not show audited financial statements to Antigua's parliament. The government-owned Bank of Antigua, the main commercial bank, was insolvent.

In this small world arrived Allen Stanford bearing gifts. To the financially strapped regime, he presented himself as a savior. He was happy to help out. He'd give them loans and help develop the islands' great tourist potential. He started by buying the troubled Bank of Antigua for $50 million. The fact that he had this amount of money shows the surprising success of the CD sales.

Upon receiving the money, the Antiguan government quickly provided him with a permit for a new bank. This was just in time to replace the Montserrat license; one can see why he would spend $50 million to get Antiguan help. This transaction no doubt widened the hole in CD assets, but it saved his golden-egg-lying goose.

So he moved Guardian International to Antigua and explained to depositors and CD sales people that he wanted to be in a location less bothered by hurricanes — he mentioned damage from Hurricane Hugo in 1989.

In the bank's annual report he dated the decision to leave Montserrat so that it seemed to be made before the letter notifying him that he was going to lose his license. He changed the bank's name from Guardian to Stanford International, probably to distance the new version from the questions that stalked the previous version.

Antigua having provided legal residency for him and his staff, he increasingly spent his time in the Caribbean, leaving his wife behind in Texas. This had multiple advantages. It could help reduce his tax liability in the United States, something he was especially concerned about after the IRS bill for 1990. It allowed him to hang out with government bigwigs and establish himself as a power on the islands. The arrangement also let him live freely with mistresses in Florida and the West Indies, while keeping up with his wife during frequent trips to Houston.

Through the companies he created he lent large sums to the government. By 2004, Antigua owed so much to Stanford's companies that this debt was close to half of the country's annual tax revenue. Some of the loans were secured by taxes and the medical fund, so Stanford was sure to be repaid.

But he did not expect to get back certain other outlays, at least not directly in money terms. He helped officials with their personal finances — took care of big expenses and provided loans that were not repaid. He wrote checks to favored politicians as campaign donations or loans.

In one instance in 1992, he lent $30,000 to the minister of finance, at the time the regulator of banks. The minister never paid this back and Stanford had it recorded as a political contribution. Later the same minister received another $100,000.

Stanford struck up a friendship with Lester Bird. When Bird feared he was suffering a heart attack, Stanford rented a private medical evacuation plane to fly him to a high-end hospital in Houston and paid the bills for the plane and hospital, which came to $48,000. He provided the government with stately new offices.

Antiguans wanted to build a modern hospital. In 1994, Stanford agreed to be the lead financer and Bird turned the project over to him. Stanford gave a loan to pay for the initial architecture and engineering costs and selected the contractors. All in all he spent more than $40 million to build the hospital, channeling the money through the Bank of Antigua.

The Antiguan press ran stories of sleaze and Stanford's influence. In one 1995 article the writer asked the key question: how did Stanford get the $40 million, given that the perennially near-bankrupt Bank of Antigua was in no position to make big loans?[15] After becoming part of Stanford's empire, the Bank of Antigua did not publish its financial statements and the government did not enforce the disclosure rule. The level of corruption in the hospital project was such that the US Congress investigated.

Stanford bought the largest Antiguan newspaper, obviously to reduce the bad press and make sure he was written about in the manner he wished. He ended up owning two newspapers in the West Indies, which gave him some control not only of news coverage of his own concerns but also of the local politics.

In 1999 he financed Lester Bird's re-election campaign. That year he became a dual citizen of Antigua and the United States.

There were persistent complaints about Lester Bird's grants of land to Stanford, who took over the precious area around VC Bird International Airport. One of the structures he built near the airport was a gleaming white Palladian villa on a gentle hill, the road going up to the door lined with verdant lawns and palm trees.

Entering the building, you went through a high portico of classical columns, topped with a pediment emblazoned with the Stanford company crest, a stylized eagle. On either side of the portico are wings with more columns, balconies and pediments. It's a striking image of contrasts: symmetrical classical lines amid pretty pink flowers, the palm trees' dark fronds against dazzling white stucco.

Inside was the lynchpin of the burgeoning financial kingdom—Stanford International Bank, started with assets transferred from Montserrat. If the value reported for Guardian International's deposits at the end of its existence were correct, Stanford brought with him nearly $100 million, but that does not account for the "hole" or his purchase of the Bank of Antigua.[16] Near the Stanford bank was the office of his newspaper, the *Antigua Sun*.

There can be no question that the move to Antigua was extremely shrewd, though caused by trouble in Montserrat. Stanford could not have chosen better than a place sorely in need of capital and run by a corruptible government. The islands suited him just so.

What he knew and liked to do was to develop luxury properties. Antigua and Barbuda offered him opportunities that would be hard to match. They contained lovely bays ideal for mooring yachts and pristine little islands off the main islands. Facilities to serve tourists were all that was needed.

In the impoverished economy his money bought more than it could have elsewhere in the Caribbean or in Florida. Just as important, Stanford was the only fish in a small pond. Elsewhere there were other powerful players; he would have faced competition and challenge. Here he had the ear of the prime minister.

So he created a construction company, hired architects and proceeded to build a tourism industry. He spiffed up Antiguan resorts and built new facilities. To make it easier for tourists to fly in, he invested in and ran two Caribbean airlines. The development around the airport included a hotel, a fancy fitness club – he clearly had a thing for gyms – and restaurants with extensive wine lists.

One vast eatery was named the Sticky Wicket, an expression from cricket, meaning a wet, muddy field. Stanford took an interest in the sport, which was languishing, and conceived a plan for its future. He would provide it with money and infrastructure.

Soon, passengers arriving at the airport were greeted by a cricket stadium that bore his name and was home to his team. So there was Stanford bank and Stanford stadium. The Sticky Wicket restaurant served meals to valued customers and political allies, who could stay at Stanford's hotel and work out at his gym. But it was hard to get enough tourists to fill the expensive facilities.

Stanford came to own a substantial chunk of Antigua. He was the largest employer after the government; a large segment of the population was on his payroll. Political powers-that-be depended on his largess. The Attorney General of Antigua was his lawyer for local legal matters.

He sponsored splashy events like Antigua Sailing Week. Talented cricket players were his protégés. The staff of the main newspaper were his employees. He created jobs in construction and tourism. He was popular, though some Antiguans disliked what he did to their country.

Stories of corruption surfaced every now and then. According to a newspaper article in November 2003, Stanford was accused of bribing two Antiguan officials – one of them the finance minister mentioned above – to the tune of $100,000 each. He wanted their cooperation in a desirable land swap. Asked about this, he was defiant and replied that he would give another $200,000 to each of the two ministers. At the time he apparently felt safe enough to treat the accusation as a joke.

Baldwin Spencer, the head of the opposition party, complained that Stanford had a lien on the whole country and called him a "modern-day colonialist."[17] By way of deflecting critics, Stanford pointed out that he did not always get his way in Antigua. There was a court battle over a hotel he coveted in dazzlingly beautiful Half Moon Bay. In 2002 the Lester Bird government tried to take the property from its American owner in order to turn it over to Stanford. The United States indicated its displeasure. Complicated legal wrangling ensued.[18]

Stanford said he loved being in Antigua, loved the country. He had done much for it — the construction he financed, the jobs he created, the sports events he sponsored. All this, and of course those bribes and kickbacks he paid politicians, helped make it a haven for him. Antigua was his realm, where he need not fear a repetition of the Montserrat blowup. No wonder he loved it.

Door off Hinges

Despite the island sanctuary he created for himself, Stanford was not immune to trouble from his country of origin. Various arms of the US government kept investigating his business on and off.[19] The specific issue of concern varied. In the early 1990s the question was where the money came from.

There was a constant flow of large amounts of cash from unknown foreign investors — some of it literally in bags, not as checks or bank wires that could be traced. Who were Stanford's clients? The suspicions that led to the 1989 investigation of the Montserrat bank arose about its Antiguan successor as well.

In 1991 there was another effort to look for evidence of narcotics connections. US Customs searched Stanford's private plane when he flew back from the Caribbean.

He must have guessed or heard that some of his staff were spying for the government. After the plane search, he fired a group of employees who may have provided information to the authorities. US Customs officers in San Antonio were concerned about possible drug smuggling by Stanford or his associates. In September 1992 the FBI sent an agent to London to investigate his activities abroad.

While no drug money laundering or smuggling case was made against him, the suspicions never went away. Stanford "stayed very prominently on the radar for years" a former FBI agent is quoted as saying. "There was a series of investigations. Obviously none of them ever ended in indictments. But we're talking various FBI field divisions, with multiple agents, then multiple agencies."[20]

At least five separate inquiries were launched. The misgivings were compounded by the Antiguan government's ill repute and the Lester Bird clique's rumored willingness to allow fraud and money laundering. As an ever growing number of offshore banks were domiciled on the island, there were calls for the US to take action.

Stanford felt threatened and decided to do something to clean up Antigua's image as rogue financial center. In 1996, he had his associates send Lester Bird a letter describing the steps the government could take to reform the banking sector.

The next year the prime minister appointed a committee to draw up a financial reform plan. Stanford himself was the chairman. The committee in turn created a task force to review banks licensed in Antigua, ostensibly to ensure their legality and make recommendations to strengthen the rules.

Stanford chose the members of this task force. They were all his associates, paid liberally by him for their services. Three were his outside lawyers and several worked for his American auditor. When they visited Antigua, some of them stayed in housing he owned.

This task force danced delicately around an issue of paramount importance to Stanford, namely how much Antigua would cooperate when a foreign government wanted action taken against a financial firm. It warned against "overly aggressive enforcement actions" that would endanger the wealth of Antiguan businesses and citizens. The resulting report contained a suggestion that only the most serious crimes warranted cooperation with a foreign government; mere allegations of fraud were not enough.

So if perchance the US demanded action against Allen Stanford, Antiguan officials could rightfully claim that their rules did not allow cooperation because the accusations were not sufficiently serious.

For a while, Antigua's chief banking overseer was an independent minded woman named Althea Crick. She declined a free airline upgrade from Stanford for a trip to Europe and discouraged his attempts to influence regulators. He got her out of the way temporarily by having her sent off on a round of tours in the Caribbean.

Crick refused to give him the confidential bank exam records he demanded. So one night he sent men to the regulator's office, they took the door off its hinges and seized the file cabinets that contained bank records. The documents were taken to his office and copied. Crick resigned.

As part of the supposed reform, a new regulator called the International Financial Sector Authority came into existence. Stanford was named chairman of this Authority's board of directors. His Antiguan lawyer – the country's Attorney General – was a member, as was one of his American lawyers. Thus Stanford and his attorneys became the regulators of his bank.

The arrangement posed so colossal and obvious a conflict of interest that it is hard to find any comparison. Bernard Madoff had connections to US regulators and advised them about market rules, but his influence on the US Securities and Exchange Commission was nothing compared to Stanford's total control of the Antiguan regulator.

These maneuvers did not escape the notice of US government observers. A cable from an American embassy in the Caribbean to the State Department said there was a "power grab" and Stanford was likely to have troublesome evidence in his record destroyed. The memo informed Washington that "the high-powered legal and investigative hired guns from the US are likely being tasked with cleansing the files to make sure there is nothing in them that could damage or implicate the American offshore banker."[21]

In 1999 the Treasury Department's Financial Crimes Enforcement Network issued a warning to banks and other financial firms that the Antiguan government had significantly weakened its banking laws and regulatory agencies. Therefore banking transactions involving Antigua merited increased scrutiny. This advisory drew attention to the Antiguan regulator's lack of independence and the conflicts of interest of its directors. The changes Stanford spearheaded were described as weakening anti-money-laundering laws and undermining efforts to fight crime.

The Antiguan International Financial Sector Authority was replaced by a body called the Financial Services Regulatory Commission. This re-naming looks like a move to simply re-brand the regulator because it had become heavily tainted. Somehow the US Treasury was sufficiently reassured to lift its warning.

The man appointed in 2003 to head the new version of the island nation's regulator was Leroy King, a long-time bank executive and former ambassador from Antigua to the United States. Stanford suggested him for the job. They were friends and King also belonged to the group around Lester Bird.

Looks Like a Ponzi Scheme

Initially the Stanford bank catered almost exclusively to well-to-do Latin Americans — even as late as 2005, around 90% of the clients were from central and south America. Ever ravenous for more funds, Stanford sought new markets for his CDs. The United States is the largest single market for financial products.

But the unlicensed sales offices he established in Texas and Florida in the 1980s for Guardian International had caused him legal headaches and now he was under watch. If he wanted to operate in America, he had no choice but to create a setup that would pass muster.

He went ahead and founded his namesake Group Company in Houston. In 1995 this entity registered with the US Securities and Exchange both as a broker-dealer of securities and as an investment adviser. Thereby for the first time Stanford and his business came under the scrutiny of the American financial overseer, specifically the Fort Worth office of the SEC.

It was a bold step, carrying a real risk that he'd run into trouble with the regulators. He likely presumed any problems would be manageable — if he thought about it at all.

In time he built an intricate web of some 130 to 140 companies that spanned North and South America and Europe. The companies were all owned – directly or more often indirectly – by him. The businesses included Stanford Coins & Bullion, construction outfits and real estate developers, but most were regional sales offices variously called Stanford Financial, Group or Trust.

While the network grew complicated because of the relations between the numerous firms, when you got down to it the business model was simple.

Stanford International Bank issued CDs; brokers and financial advisers who worked out of offices mostly in the Caribbean, the Southern United States and Latin America sold those CDs. The proceeds were supposedly invested in low-risk securities and bullion by skilled money managers.

The primary function of Stanford Group Company in Houston, like most of the other companies, was to sell the CDs that originated from Antigua. Soon the Houston office became a sales powerhouse, responsible for retailing about half the CDs issued by the bank.

This broker-dealer did the required paperwork and submitted to the SEC its audited reports. The report for the fiscal year ending in June 1997 caught the attention of a branch chief at the SEC Fort Worth office, an examiner by the name of Julie Preuitt.[22] She noticed that the firm had gone from little revenue to a huge amount of revenue in a short time, an unusual pattern. What is more, the business model looked implausible.

Superficially, the reason for the fast growth was obvious. Stanford's certificates always offered higher interest rates compared to CDs from American banks. The difference was not huge — two to four percentage points. For instance, Stanford paid 5.375% on a 3-year CD at a time when US bank CDs paid less than 3.2%. Still, it was enough of a draw for some investors.

Stanford credited his bank's low costs, in particular the tax savings from being domiciled in Antigua, for the better rates. In addition, the bank's underlying investments were said to be highly profitable, with part of the gains passed on to CD holders. The reported returns for Stanford International Bank's portfolio never went below double-digits for some fifteen years.

Davis now oversaw the financial and organizational aspects of the whole set of companies. Davis did not resemble Wall Street chief financial officers. He lived in a small town in Mississippi, commuting to the Stanford office in Memphis via a company jet.

People were often surprised when Davis began meetings with a prayer. Sometimes he started phone conversations with a prayer, too. For a while he taught Sunday school at the First Baptist Church in Baldwyn, Miss. He and his wife ran a bible study group. There Davis met a perky young girl named Laura Pendergest.

After she graduated from Mississippi State University, Pendergest was hired by Davis and rose fast in the Stanford company.[23] She and Davis had an affair for three years. Informed about this relationship, Stanford said it was good, she would be loyal.[24] In 2003 Pendergest became the chief investment officer of the company, apparently after the affair with Davis ended.

So the attractive young protégé came to preside over the outside managers who traded securities for the portfolio. As investment chief, she had the help of a group of financial analysts to pick and monitor the portfolio managers. But the analysts were not necessarily experienced. Many were relatives and follow church members hired by Davis and Pendergest.[25]

Sales people and printed brochures assured clients that the Stanford companies were authorized and overseen by both the SEC and the brokerage industry's self regulator. The latter, originally called NASD, became the Financial Industry Regulatory Authority – or FINRA – in 2007 after merging with a department of the New York Stock Exchange. This industry supervisor, itself subject to the SEC, came to play a critical role in conflicts between Stanford and employees of his brokerage.

Besides the oversight of the two regulatory bodies, there was the matter of insurance. Potential buyers of CDs would be discouraged if it occurred to them that unlike American banks the Stanford bank, being offshore, was not protected by FDIC. To get around that barrier, sales personnel gave the impression that the Stanford CDs were backed by another public entity, the Securities Investor Protection Corporation (SIPC), set up by Congress to protect brokerage customers. The fine print in some of the sales materials said there was no SIPC coverage, but the disclaimer was easy to miss.

The bank could buy private insurance for the deposits. That, however, is very expensive. So in 1991 Allen Stanford concocted a fake insurance policy. He joked to the marketing executive whose help he enlisted that it was amazing, the risks people were willing to take for an extra two percent return on their CD. Sales people and depositors were shown copies of the phony policy.

A big potential investor wanted to make sure there was an insurance company behind this policy. Thereupon Stanford created a shell company, rented an office cubicle in London and had Davis fly there for a day to fax a confirmation from this supposed insurer. Later, as the CDs brought more money, Stanford did buy a small amount of insurance from Lloyd's of London. This was touted about as evidence that the CDs were secure.

In 1997 the SEC examiner Preuitt did not know about these maneuvers. And she had no details as to how the claimed returns were achieved — neither did the brokers and investment advisers who sold the CDs. But she could see immediately that these were not like regular CDs issued by American banks.

Also, she noticed that brokers, though free to sell other products, were given big bonuses for selling the CDs. That meant they had an incentive to push the CDs whether or not these were right for a client.

Preuitt decided that the high commissions paid to the broker-dealer network for selling the CDs were evidence that these could not be legitimate investments. Suspecting fraud, she asked an experienced accountant to examine the Houston brokerage.

Another SEC officer, Mary Lou Felsman, an assistant district administrator at the Fort Worth examination program, looked at the exceptional returns the bank claimed to generate and realized these were very unlikely to come from the conservative approach described in the marketing materials. Another red flag was the broker-dealer's failure to keep records for the CD sales.

Something else was odd. In 1996, Allen Stanford had personally put $19 million into the business. Preuitt and Felsman noticed that around that time Stanford International Bank gave loans totaling $19 million to him and a separate company he owned. They suspected that the money came from the bank's customers—Stanford was possibly stealing from investors.

The company's counsel replied that Stanford invested his personal money, not CD proceeds. Had this matter been further pursued, perhaps Allen would have mentioned the legacy he received from Lodis via his father and their real estate wealth as the source of the money. But it did not come to that.

SEC examiners are an advance guard in search of violations. When they spot problems, they refer the case to the enforcement division for the next step, which is to use subpoena power to force the subject of the investigation to testify and give requested information. Stanford was not about to cooperate voluntarily; he had to be subpoenaed through an enforcement action.

Both Preuitt and Felsman were concerned that this was a fraudulent scheme. The above-market returns looked "absolutely ludicrous" to them. The Fort Worth examiners went as far as they could go within their authority. They warned in a 1997 report on Stanford of "Possible misrepresentations. Possible Ponzi scheme." They recorded these issues in the SEC internal tracking system and sent the report to enforcement.

Felsman retired at the end of 1997. At that time there had been no action against the Houston broker-dealer. As she left, Felsman advised Preuitt: "keep your eye on these people because this looks like a Ponzi scheme to me and some day it's going to blow up."[26]

On the basis of this history of Preuitt and Felsman, you have to be favorably impressed by the SEC. These skilled and alert examiners quickly figured out what Stanford was up to and urged action to stop him. One could not ask for better performance. Obviously they were highly competent as well as conscientious in their work.

The examiners did exactly what a regulator is supposed to do, serving the public well. Surely this was taxpayers' money well spent.

But the response from the rest of the bureaucracy and other parts of the government creates an altogether different impression.

Green Light

Despite the serious warnings, the SEC enforcement group let the matter rest for the next eight months. There was no further investigation of what Stanford was doing with the CD money. But in May 1998 US Customs contacted the SEC about the Houston broker-dealer. The issue of drug trafficking and money laundering had come up again.

A narcotics investigation by the Drug Enforcement Administration found that the Mexican Juárez drug cartel was passing its money through the Stanford bank. An SEC attorney attended a meeting of law enforcement officers in Houston to discuss this development. A long list of agencies and departments were concerned, from the US Attorney's Office, the Postal Inspector and the Secret Service to the State Department and Treasury.

In 1999 Stanford handed the Juárez money – $3 million – to the US government. This had a bizarre consequence, namely a lawsuit in Florida against Stanford filed by parties identified in the media as front men for a Mexican drug lord. They charged Stanford with failing to protect their money when he gave it to the Drug Enforcement Administration.[27] They sounded disappointed.

Otherwise there was no obvious legal repercussion for Stanford and his business from the Juárez incident. Yet evidence accumulated. Another source, the Texas securities regulator, gave the FBI and SEC information about money laundering at the Stanford bank.[28] Neither bureaucracy acted on this.

How did Stanford get off so lightly? It was reported that he not only turned over the money but provided information to the US about his customers in the narcotics trade and flows of illegal funds.

BBC News reported that starting in 1999 he became an informer for the Drug Enforcement Administration, citing sources close to that agency.[29] Hence he obtained the protection of the DEA. Given his extensive international contacts and constant travelling around the world, he probably was a valuable spy.

Asked in interviews whether he played this role, Stanford refused to answer. As for the drug money deposited in his bank, he suggested those were minor incidents for such a large, global financial operation. The DEA declined to comment.

Meanwhile, the one dogged pursuer of Stanford kept at it. The SEC examination group had a go at the Houston company from another angle. This time they looked at its registered investment advisers.

Advisers have a legal duty to recommend investments appropriate for each client's financial condition. But the Stanford investment advisers told the SEC examiner they knew little about the portfolio.

Without enough information behind their recommendations, the advisers were on the face of it violating their legal obligation to customers. "It just smells bad," the examiner concluded.

Reflecting the findings, the SEC sent a letter to the Stanford company warning that "Any departure from this fiduciary standard may constitute fraud upon clients..."

Among the officials who received the 1997 report on a possible Ponzi scheme at the broker-dealer as well as the 1998 report on dereliction of duty by the investment advisers was the assistant director of the enforcement program at the SEC Fort Worth office. This was a lawyer named Spencer Barasch. Initially he would not start an inquiry. But after the money laundering issue was brought to the SEC by other federal agencies, his office took action.[30]

To fight what looked like a serious threat, Stanford had on his side an attorney who possessed inside knowledge and connections. Wayne Secore, previously the head of the SEC Fort Worth office, now represented Stanford Group. Having been there, he understood how regulators did things and also knew some of the SEC staff involved in the inquiry.

Stanford's lawyers requested a meeting between Secore and Barasch. What transpired between the former regulator and the current supervisor of the inquiry against his client became a question of some interest.

What's certain is that Barash shut down the inquiry only three months after it started. He did this knowing that it would shock and disappoint his examiner colleagues. After all, their reports stated that this was a possible Ponzi scheme.

Concerned that Preuitt would not take the news well, he called her and told her the matter was closed due to "some problems with the case."[31]

According to Preuitt, Barash told her that he decided not to pursue the inquiry further after his conversation with Secore. Barash had asked Secore if there was a case against Stanford and Secore had told him there was not. Thus reassured, the enforcement assistant director stopped the process. No subpoenas were issued to get information about how the money from the CDs was being invested.

Later Barash testified that he only vaguely recalled Secore in the role of Stanford's attorney and denied that he was influenced by Secore in this matter. Given the conflicting accounts by Preuitt and Barash, it is not clear why he stopped the inquiry. When the matter was investigated, Barash and others gave numerous explanations.

Some of the supposed reasons for not pursuing the case were obviously questionable. Thus the excuse that the CD issuer was a foreign bank outside US jurisdiction and the investors were not Americans. When they looked at the investment advisers, the SEC examiners had found that the clients did include a few Americans by 1998. But the more important fact was that Stanford was soliciting an ever larger number of American investors.

Another reason given for quashing the inquiry, namely that the company would not provide information and answer questions, should have led to greater suspicion rather than less. That should be cause for investigating more aggressively and issuing subpoenas, not for pulling back.

The main point, however, was that taking on Stanford was too tough. Barash said he had been told by senior SEC officials to focus on accounting problems and there was pressure to bring a lot of cases, which meant a preference for easier targets.

Stanford, of course, took care to make himself a difficult target. One way he did this was by hiring Secore, thereby getting the benefit of the erstwhile regulator's expertise and contacts inside the SEC Fort Worth office.

Barash indicated that in 1998 he referred the matter to the brokerage industry self-regulator NASD. No evidence could be found of the referral. In any event, NASD and its successor FINRA dealt with small violations, not with major fraud. A decade would pass before FINRA cited the Stanford companies, and then it did so for mostly minor infractions and assessed penalties that were trivial for a business of the size.

The end of the SEC inquiry meant that Stanford was home free after being investigated by various arms of the US government. He was not charged with any crime, whether money laundering or fraud. He had been vetted by the SEC more than once, both his broker-dealer and investment adviser operation had been examined and he had emerged with no blemish on his official public record. No action was taken by NASD.

In effect, he had a green light to go ahead. His brash decision had paid off. By 2000, his headquarters in Houston contained a sizable sales staff. In time he opened 25 or more regional offices in the United States, pushing the CDs to Americans looking to invest their retirement money.

The chasm between the bank's reported assets and actual liabilities continued to widen; Davis continued to create the false books and records Stanford demanded. The value of the investment portfolio was adjusted every year to produce the desired return.

Later, Davis said he repeatedly warned Stanford that what they were doing would have consequences, and not good consequences — demonstrating what he meant by putting his hands together as if handcuffed. Stanford would laugh and say he was going to blame it all on Davis.[32]

That sounds like a joke but turned out to be something of a warning. In fact Stanford did blame Davis when the handcuffs became reality. Why did Davis, seemingly a more cautious man than his old roommate, go on producing false records? Why did he not leave?

Part of the answer seems to be that Davis was under the influence of Stanford, who used flattery and money to control people but sometimes also fear and intimidation.[33] He bullied Davis, ordered him not to talk to anyone (including his wife) about the bank's secret and told him off for doing anything on his own, even rearranging employees' offices.

On one occasion he demonstrated his recklessness by taking Davis for a drive in his new Mercedes-Benz, going at 170 miles an hour. Had Davis wanted to leave, Stanford would have threatened to wreck his career and probably done so.

But that was not all. Davis was used to the wealth and high position, which he could not get elsewhere. For a while, there was the relationship with Pendergest. Moreover, he had already dirtied his hands. If the thing blew up, it would be on his head as well as his chief's.

The Congressional Record

In the 1990s Stanford built political influence in the Caribbean. Early in the next decade, a specific threat to his interest appears to have drawn his attention to Washington. An anti-money-laundering bill was introduced in US Congress, requiring offshore banks to provide information to federal authorities regarding the sources of their funds.

Within a few months Stanford hired multiple lobbyists to work against the proposed legislation. In 2001 the bill went to a Senate committee, where it quietly disappeared.

By that time he had an expanding business established on American soil. The SEC and FBI investigations had gone nowhere but nevertheless shown that he was vulnerable. Having influence in Antigua was not enough; he needed allies in America. So he endeavored to build US connections, sparing neither expense nor effort to cultivate long-term relationships with government people.

Whenever legislation came up in Congress that could lead to greater scrutiny of his bank in Antigua or business in America, he donated openhandedly to both parties and put up a fight. After the September 2001 attacks on New York and Washington, the US government went after illegal funds and Stanford could no longer block anti-money laundering measures. But he was successful in killing other proposals.[34]

In 2002 he paid for lobbying against a bill that would have allowed state and federal regulators to share details of fraud cases. This might have led regulators to connect his current CDs to Guardian Bank's earlier violation of bank laws in Texas, Florida and California.

That year he donated large sums, including $800,000 to the Democratic Senatorial Campaign Committee. Before long, the antifraud network bill vanished.

In time Stanford developed ties to a wide circle of both marquee political names and behind-the-scenes operators. In cultivating American politicians, he made extensive use of his Caribbean connections and properties. Thanks to his patronage, US Representatives went on junkets to "study" Caribbean economic development in attractive settings.

He spirited them off on his private jets to luxury resorts, entertained them at the Sticky Wicket and other high-end restaurants and introduced them to local bigwigs. They could eat lobster, hobnob with a prime minister and drink toasts to Stanford.

Thus in 2003, seven Congressmen flew to Antigua on two of Stanford's planes. Among those who enjoyed the financier's hospitality on that occasion were Gregory Meeks, a Democrat from New York, and Bob Ney, a Republican from Ohio. The trip, which cost Stanford almost $40,000, led to the founding of the Caribbean Caucus in Congress. In the years to come, he would provide campaign financing as well as expenses-paid Caribbean jaunts to members of this group.

Both Meeks and Ney served on the House Committee on Financial Services. The same names received funding from a non-profit organization called the Inter-American Economic Council. In 2005, Stanford provided 85% of the financing for this entity, which functioned as a conduit for his money, a front for his interests and a boost to his good name. It paid for 11 trips to the region by Caribbean Caucus members.

Some took even more frequent advantage of Stanford's beneficence. Tom DeLay, at one time the Republican leader of the House, used Stanford's jets at least 16 times. Later DeLay was convicted of illegally scheming to channel campaign contributions to candidates for the Texas legislature and sentenced to three years in prison. Stanford donated to the legal defense fund and DeLay's attorney, Dick DeGuerin, advised the financier on his own troubles with the law.

Certain associates showed up as bit players in later scandals. Thus one of the lobbyists Stanford paid in 2002 was John Wyma, subsequently an aide to Illinois governor Rod Blagojevich.[35] The latter became infamous for his bald attempt to sell to whoever provided the greatest benefit to himself the Senate seat vacated by Barack Obama. Wyma became news fodder because he recorded his conversations with the governor, evidence that helped send Blagojevich to prison.

The beneficiaries of Stanford's gifts showed their gratitude in a variety of ways, some substantial, others symbolic. Ney inserted into the *Congressional Record* a statement that "Allen R. Stanford has been recognized as the 2006 Recipient of the 'Excellence in Leadership Award' by the Inter-American Economic Council" and "acknowledged for his performance and leadership in the areas of finance and investments."[36]

Thereupon Stanford made another campaign donation to Ney, who however was not long for politics. Implicated in the Abramoff lobbying scandal, he too went to prison. Stanford demonstrated his loyalty to the fallen politician by contributing to the legal defense fund, as he did for DeLay.

He performed all kinds of nice deeds for his politician friends, like hosting a wedding dinner in Antigua for a member of the Caribbean Caucus.

An attendee of the 2003 junket and recipient of donations would show his own devotion to Stanford when the latter was accused of fraud. "I love you and believe in you," this Congressman wrote in a message to his besieged friend. "If you want my ear/voice — e-mail.".[37]

In addition to his direct contacts with US Representatives and Senators, by 2005 Stanford had on retainer a well-known lobbyist. This was Ben Barnes, a former Lieutenant Governor of Texas and a fellow real estate magnate. A protégé of Lyndon Johnson early in his career, Barnes was a top fundraiser and influential Democrat, though touches of scandal cut short his time as elected officeholder.[38] A large donor himself, he was also a champion collector of donations from others, a big "bundler" for John Kerry's presidential campaign.

Barnes advised Stanford on his political contributions, suggesting that he give more to Democrats as that party gained greater control. Routine procedure for business interests in Washington is to hedge their bets by donating to both parties. But it is also common practice to adjust the political mix somewhat when there is a shift in power — thus Exxon Mobil, with one of the largest lobbying operations, appointed a Democratic director to its K Street office upon the Democratic triumph in the 2008 election.[39]

Stanford always cultivated numerous Democrats and Republicans, giving alike to the inaugural committee of George W. Bush and the Presidential campaign of Barack H. Obama. He wooed and networked across the political spectrum. He, his companies and associates contributed about $2 million to legislators ranging from left-wing Democrats Charles Ranger and Barney Frank to Republican presidential candidate John McCain.

Separately, larger sums went to the Congressional committees of both parties. But on the whole Stanford spent more on Democrats—for instance, more than ten times as much for the Democratic Senatorial Campaign Committee as the National Republican Senatorial Committee.[40] In addition to such direct contributions, he channeled another $5 million to $10 million to lobbyists.[41]

The Democrat Barnes remained his top political adviser and was well compensated for his help.[42] While Barnes looked after several issues that affected his client, he lobbied in particular about a significant tax matter. Holding dual citizenship in Antigua and America, Stanford remained subject to US taxes. Some time in the 2000s he officially became a resident of St. Croix in the US Virgin Islands.

How much he actually lived in St. Croix is unclear, though he purchased an estate there. In later years he sailed back and forth to Antigua and other points in the Caribbean on the larger of his two yachts—named Sea Eagle and Little Eagle. If he wanted, he could sail for a long time without making landfall, having acquired a tugboat to ferry supplies to the yacht. And he spent a lot of time flying around the world, touching down for short stays in Latin America, Asia and Europe.

But by officially residing in St. Croix – rather than in Miami, where he owned a mansion, or Houston, where the US company was headquartered – he paid much less American income tax. The tax rate for the US Virgin Islands was in effect only 3.5%.

Naturally Stanford wanted to make sure Congress did not increase this rate. His allies succeeded in preserving the low tax.[43] But he further hankered to get the rule expanded so that he could apply the low rate to his income from all offshore sources. To his disappointment that did not happen.

Of course, the public argument for the special low tax in the US Virgin Islands and its proposed expansion to income from other regions sounded perfectly respectable. It would promote economic development on the islands, attracting people and investment. Lobbyists spread the word of the economic benefits. That it helped Allen Stanford pay less taxes was a little known consequence, possibly unintended by policymakers when the original law was passed.

So for a time Stanford managed to legally pay a much lower tax rate than most middle-class Americans. But he did not confine himself to legal tax strategies. He furthermore illegally hid some of his income and paid no tax at all on it.

It took the Internal Revenue Service many years to catch up — to calculate that he personally owed $432 million in federal back taxes, including interest and penalties, for the period from 1999 to 2003. By the time that tax bill arrived, it was the least of his problems.

Barnes provided other services as well. Stanford wanted to import a Cuban team to play at the cricket tournament he organized in Antigua. Barnes lobbied to get government permission and consulted about the tournament. He advised Stanford on his various projects, such as the development of an island off Antigua and clean energy investments.

In media interviews, Stanford professed to take a great interest in environmental problems and even recommended a book on the topic. He touted his eco-friendliness. Perhaps he hoped to get a clean energy subsidy from American taxpayers via his many friends in Congress.

The Castle and Sir Allen

As his business grew, Stanford tried to move away from its suspicion-raising origins. He took measures to distance himself from the persistent suggestions of drug money laundering and sleaze that dogged him. Although the taint never entirely went away, he succeeded in creating the public image of a legitimate financier.

His American political connections helped burnish his name. CD clients would receive cheerful performance reports bound in embossed fake leather. To add to the reassurance, congratulatory remarks from public officials were quoted and honors such as the commendation in the *Congressional Record* mentioned. Sometimes there was a photo of Stanford posing with a well-known politician, both grinning, with a caption describing the happy occasion for the photo shoot.

The customers looking at the pictures and endorsements could not but help be impressed. "We saw photos of our Senators and Congressmen with Allen Stanford," said a client later. "We even received a copy of a letter from President George W. Bush applauding the Stanford Financial Group in 2008."[44] The manager of their nest egg was not just anyone—he associated with and was approved by the highest dignitaries in Washington!

Thus Stanford received multiple benefits from his political outlays. His allies not only protected his interest in the legislature but also enhanced his respectability.

The Republican president was featured in Stanford's propaganda but when the top political names changed, there was Stanford with the new crowd. The same year he got the letter from Bush, the *Antigua Sun* published the photo of Sir Allen with then-Senator Barack Obama. With the political winds turning, Democrats came to the fore in his publicity campaign and received more goodies from him

In 2006 he boosted his name in another way by finagling a knighthood. He claimed he had been given the title by the Queen and knighted by Prince Edward, but that was not correct—he was knighted by an Antiguan official. Antigua's status as a member of the British Commonwealth gave its government the right to bestow titles. The prince happened to be visiting the island at the time.

The full title was Knight Commander of the Most Distinguished Order of the Nation of Antigua and Barbuda, an impressive mouthful. The British press mocked the pretension. Undeterred, Stanford insisted people call him Sir Allen, on occasion telling off those who forgot to put the "Sir" in front of his name.

He financed numerous sports events not only in Antigua and America but also in Britain. Thus he sponsored the Charity Polo Day at the Royal Military Academy Sandhurst— Prince Harry played in the Stanford Sandhurst Cup.[45] While polo, sailing and golf continued to receive contributions, cricket became his favorite.

This was not the game traditionally played, which did not appeal to him because it is slow and takes a long time. What he promoted was a new, faster, shorter form of cricket. British sportswriters were often critical of the newfangled version.

But Stanford paid large sums to talented players and assembled his own team – the Stanford Superstars – to play the new game. Eventually he started a series of matches under a $100 million agreement with the English Cricket Board. Cricket boards in the West Indies received funds to develop their teams and participate in contests he organized .

He even had people from his company audit the spending of this money, to make sure it was used for the intended purpose. So a journalist was told and reported in an admiring story. Here was a grand patron of the sports enforcing honesty everywhere.[46] This was one of the gestures Stanford made to demonstrate his anti-corruption credentials.

The seeming obsession with things English went beyond the knighthood and cricket. His offices were decorated in the style of old-fashioned London men's clubs with worn leather couches, mahogany bookcases, Oriental rugs, and in at least one conference room, paintings of traditional hunting scenes.

Even his Texas drawl took on vague British inflections, possibly the influence of his long-time English girlfriend. He met the striking brunette, Louise Sage, in London.[47] Soon afterwards, he sent a private jet to bring her to America. The relationship lasted 12 years and produced two children.

In 2003, Stanford acquired a 57-room mansion in a Miami suburb. A fantasy of medieval architecture with turrets and a moat in the midst of vast tropical gardens, Tyecliffe Castle was a fitting home for a man who aspired to knighthood — though he did not have the title yet.

For a short while he lived in the castle with his English mistress and their children, at least when he was not sailing the Caribbean, prowling around the world to push CD sales or enjoying the charms of other women.

But the fairytale trappings were not enough to smooth the friction between Allen and Louise. She wanted to get married and even changed her name to Sage-Stanford — like two other girlfriends who took his name. He promised to marry her, once or twice even claimed to get a marriage license, but at the last minute told her he could not do it.

Certainly in a legal sense he could not marry her, being still married to his sweetheart from way back. Unknown to Louise until later, the real Mrs. Allen Stanford lived in Texas, where her husband continued to see her. Sometimes she visited him in Antigua, but he had to be careful that she did not run into his girlfriends.

Had he and Louise tied the knot, they would have had a fake marriage to go with the fake castle. But Allen did not go through the ceremony; perhaps he never intended to commit bigamy.

In time Louise learnt that he had a wife and multiple girlfriends besides and moved out of Tyecliffe Castle. The British press took to calling her and other long-term girlfriends Stanford's "outside" wives.[48] Of his six known offspring, five were not by his wife.

This much can be said for Allen — he took care of his progeny, at least financially, spending as much as a quarter-of-a-million dollars a year per child. The children flew on private planes, went to expensive private schools, were given trust funds and had fabulous holidays, including one on a 120-foot yacht off Nantucket, chartered for $100,000 a week.

Family

Family history remained a big part of Stanford's endeavor to look respectable. The website of his company told everybody about the five generations of Texans he descended from and the business inherited from Lodis that formed the basis of his wealth. Clients might be shown a film about the enterprising barber.

Allen hired genealogists to establish a link between him and Leland Stanford, the founder of Stanford University, and claimed to be the sixth twice-removed cousin. The university disputed this and sued him for trademark infringement.

When *Forbes* magazine ranked Stanford 205th on a list of 400 richest Americans and reported his net worth as $2.2 billion in September 2008, the source of this wealth was specified as "Finance, inherited and growing." The "inherited" part was emphasized in the magazine's write-up: "Dad retired 1993, gave 500-employee company to Allen..."

But there was no such company passed on to Allen. It is most curious that he told people this yarn.

As described above, the small insurance brokerage in Mexia had no direct connection to the offshore financial business. It was sold before the bank in Montserrat got going. Its sale contributed indirectly, by bringing in money that Allen and his father used to buy Texas property. That in turn helped in part finance the bank venture.

But Allen could not have built his empire without raising money from Latin Americans, by all evidence a feat he accomplished on his own. Initially he did the marketing himself; in time he hired and trained a formidable sales force. This was not a gift from his ancestors, except in the genetic sense if you think his genes made him a great marketer.

Yet he insisted on giving a substantial share of the credit to his family, making this point repeatedly in public and even grossly exaggerating his inheritance. It is unusual for an American to create a business and then attribute it largely to inheritance.

In a culture that values the accomplishments of self-made men and women, coming from middle-class or humble circumstances is often a badge of honor. Making money is the measure of an individual's success, whether one likes it or not. There is no stigma to being nouveau rich, especially if you're as rich as Stanford claimed to be.

But he kept insisting that he inherited a large portion of his fortune, that he came from old money. The false claim that his father "gave 500-employee company to Allen" was part of this campaign.

His efforts to acquire a classy veneer backfired in some ways. British journalists decried him as vulgar when he landed at the ancient Lord's Cricket Ground in London in a gleaming gold-trimmed helicopter and displayed a container filled with $20 million in fresh bills. He would distribute the money to the winning team in the new-style cricket contest he organized in Antigua.

It was taken as further proof of his crude ways when he was filmed cavorting with the pretty wives of cricket players during a match, with one of them sitting on his lap.

•

European press reports uniformly depicted him as the stereotypical Texan — big, loud and flashy. Commentators shot down his pretentions and called him a clown.[49] Nobody could possibly mistake him for a British aristocrat. In fact nobody mistook him for other than a son of Texas, however far he travelled from Mexia.

The perception that he was a buffoon was misleading. On occasion he may have acted like one, but Stanford was no fool. Maybe he enjoyed putting on old world airs, but it is not that he was sentimental about English titles, games or for that matter anything.

Cricket, polo and other sports were a way to build his brand. It was advertising. Judging from a comment he let go, he was perfectly clear as to what he was getting for the money. He affected Anglophile tastes and mannerisms because he badly wanted to acquire a patina of lineage. The title and the old-money English trappings helped make his business look solid and stable.

He did all this for the same reason he built the Palladian villa near Antigua airport to house his bank. Tall classical pillars, grand hallways, a plentitude of marble and mahogany, physically embodied the wealth he wanted to project. The structure was partly empty; the small staff occupied only part of the grand interior. But it looked imposing and helped market the product.

Same with the title, family history and patronage of the sports. No matter how thin and artificial the pretense, it was useful as long as some people were impressed and bought the CDs. All evidence suggests this was a hard man who did things for practical reasons.

Besides marketing, there may have been other reasons behind his persistent quest for distinguished ancestry. One likely explanation is highlighted by the question asked in the 1990s by an Antiguan journalist: where did the millions of dollars he spent on building the hospital come from? The financial advisers who sold the CDs asked versions of the same question, as did their clients. So did SEC examiners.

He personally gave loans to the Antiguan government, personally owned land, buildings, resorts, airlines, restaurants, newspapers, a fitness club. Were CD proceeds channeled to his businesses? Stanford always and emphatically declared that there was no connection between the CDs and his personal businesses.

Given that the CDs were supposed to be extremely safe, it would not do to have people suspect the money was financing speculative development schemes, let alone Stanford's political protection and profligate spending. He had to have some other source — hence his obsession with showing that he came from rich old stock and inherited wealth.

There is no sign of a substantial inheritance. Until the CD sales got going, Allen led a middle-class life. He flew on commercial airlines, not private jets; lived in an ordinary suburban house, not a castle. But you would have to know him from way back to notice that the outward evidence of wealth appeared only after he established the CD business.

In addition to the need to camouflage his dependence on CD revenues, there is another plausible reason for his insistence on family legacy. New money would not have been a problem; but dirty money was a sword hanging over his head.

Perhaps he wanted to cover up the smell of the cash that came in bags, that helped get the Montserrat bank off the ground and never entirely went away. It started with stories of Stanford meeting tough-looking guys in the early-to-mid 1980s and large suitcases full of cash changing hands at his office. It continued over decades with investigations of narcotics connections and money laundering.

So he emphasized his ancestors and the old family business he took over. The respectable picture would function as a smokescreen for a very different kind of family that may have helped finance his real estate ventures and bank at the beginning.

That would explain what is otherwise inexplicable, namely his quick initial success with the CDs. There has to be a special reason to put money into a brand new bank run by someone with no reassuring track record in banking. People with illegal profits do not have many options for investing; hence they can not be picky. Plus, they're used to risk. A helpful young man with an excellent laundering scheme could very well get enough capital to seed his business.

If laundering is the priority, investment returns are a secondary matter. So the fact that he was no expert in financial matters and knew next to nothing about banks, stocks or bonds would not matter — he knew enough to achieve a useful transformation of money from shady sources into eminently respectable-sounding CDs.

But once he attracted numerous clients and governments started to notice him, it would make sense for Stanford to pull away from his old partners. He was too smart to endanger his booming financial scheme.

He tried to dissociate himself and his business from the connections that helped him earlier. Over time he probably tried to clean up the money laundering act and get rid of the evidence.

He must have overlooked some remnants or was too greedy to turn away customers. When the Juárez money come up, he gave it to the Drug Enforcement Administration and became an informer. His old underground customers were disappointed and sued him — maybe they knew him from the 1980s, had been his partners in real estate deals, helped him build his CD business.

His attempt to create a new image did not entirely succeed; he remained infamous for his corrupt ways. In 2006, American diplomats in Barbados were careful not to get too close to Stanford because he was rumored to engage in "bribery, money laundering, and political manipulation."[50]

The same cable to the State Department reported that ""For his part, Stanford said he preferred to conduct his business without contacting the embassy, resolving any investment disputes directly with local governments. It is whispered in the region that Stanford facilitates resolution with significant cash contributions."

The US government has many parts and is subject to many powerful influences. No doubt Caribbean politicians were easier to deal with. Stanford could be fairly confident that they would keep their word — after all, he remained their main source of "significant cash contributions." Knowing that he needed all the protection he could get, he continued to spread the contributions around.

Among the officials who benefitted from this munificence was Leroy King. After he was appointed the head of Antigua's banking regulator under the financier's auspices, King, Stanford and another employee of the Antiguan regulatory agency performed a brotherhood "blood oath" pledging to help each other.[51]

The parties kept their oath. Stanford paid King hundreds of thousands of dollars and gave his companion a highly compensated job. Like Stanford, King was a citizen of both the US and Antigua and traveled frequently between his residences. Stanford eased the trips by providing King with the use of private jets and corporate cars and threw in goodies like Super Bowl tickets. King reciprocated by providing a special kind of service.

Despite the shadows from his past, the brand Stanford built was spectacularly successful. People worldwide wanted the unusual combination of security and high interest that he offered. They could not get that deal elsewhere; since nobody else sold practically guaranteed CDs with returns above the normal. He had a niche where he faced no serious competition. He just had to buff his brand, cultivate officials everywhere and tamp down on troublemakers.

Keep Them Hustling

When SEC examiners took another look at the Houston broker-dealer in 2002, they realized that CD sales had grown significantly in the four years since the previous examination. Even as warning signs multiplied, people everywhere were buying Stanford's product. Crucially, from a US regulator's perspective, there were many more Americans among the buyers than before.

Around this time the SEC received at least two letters from customers expressing fear of fraud. One was from an accountant in Mexico worried that her 75-year-old mother was dependent on this questionable investment. The writer was confused as to whether the CDs had FDIC protection like deposits at American banks, probably because sales pitches gave the impression that the CDs were protected in some fashion.

An SEC examiner drafted a response to the letter, asking whether the writer was willing to have it considered an official complaint. If the answer was yes, an inquiry could start and Stanford could be subpoenaed for information. But the response was never sent to the complainer in Mexico.

The draft went to Barasch, who did not approve it. Instead he referred the matter to the Texas State Securities Board — hence it was out of the hands of the SEC. So he claimed. Investigators found no evidence of this referral.

The enforcement division did not start a new inquiry and the complaints were not answered. Afterwards Barasch said he did not recall the 2002 report. Neither did he remember why he had decided not to open an inquiry.

Once they realized that their colleagues in enforcement would not pursue Stanford, the SEC examiners tried to get the Federal Reserve to investigate. After all, the CD issuer was a bank and the Federal Reserve is the banking regulator.

The Federal Reserve referred the matter to the FBI. It is not clear what, if anything, the FBI did. Perhaps the DEA protected him. Thus petered out the 2002 effort to bring Stanford to account.

The complaints did not end. In 2003 the Texas State Securities Board itself forwarded to Barasch a letter that detailed similarities between a known Ponzi scheme and the Stanford business. Among other similarities, the letter pointed to "a Byzantine corporate structure where the funds from deposits were held in off shore entities." This looked significant enough that somebody from the Texas State Securities Board called Barasch to draw his attention to the letter.

Barasch later testified that he did not remember the letter, just as he did not remember the previous complaints. During the call with the Texas State Securities official, he did not bring up the previous letters or examinations that raised similar issues.

Again in 2003 a former employee named Charles Hazlett filed a claim against the Stanford company with NASD, complaining that he was pressured to sell the CDs and fired when he refused.

Hazlett was among the many brokers the company lured away from other firms with the promise of juicy bonuses. He joined the Miami office and initially sold so many CDs that he won a BMW — one of the numerous incentives Stanford used to encourage sales.

But a client of Hazlett wanted to learn the details of how the high returns were achieved. Hazlett asked chief investment officer Pendergest, who said she could not tell him. When he insisted, she ran off sobbing and apparently complained to her patron, Davis.[52] Thereupon Davis called Hazlett and surprised him with the question, "Do you believe in God?" Davis proceeded to reprimand Hazlett.

The real question was whether Hazlett believed in Stanford and since he had become skeptical on that score, he and others like him were in conflict with the company management. Not only CD customers but the salespeople had to be kept in the dark as to what was happening to the money. When they expressed suspicion, brokers turned into a threat.

They might decide to stop pitching the CDs and pull their clients – who were often attached to the individual adviser and came with him or her to the Stanford brokerage – out. Worse, brokers might tell others that they'd been misled.

Around the same time that Hazlett went to NASD, another former employee told a NASD arbitration panel that she suspected Stanford was running a Ponzi scheme. This financial adviser, Leyla Basagoitia, pointed out the danger signals noticed by SEC examiners. There was no credible auditor and the promise of consistently high returns did not "correspond to the reality of markets."

Basagoitia told NASD the real market value of the Stanford bank's portfolio was believed to be significantly below the obligations to CD holders. While clients were assured the CDs were absolutely safe, the proceeds were going to speculative investments such as real estate.

These complaints went to the SEC as well as to NASD and were referred to Barasch. There was no action against Stanford.

NASD arbitrators ruled against the two former employees, who as a result were forced to pay Stanford large sums. Meanwhile his associates spread the word that the whistleblowers were disgruntled troublemakers. It became near impossible for them to get jobs. Hazlett had to leave the brokerage industry.

It became a pattern for the Stanford company to discredit employees who complained of fraud, slandering them so as to ruin their professional standing. That way, their allegations would carry little weight.

Their reputations were destroyed so as to minimize the threat they posed. But what happened to Stanford's skeptical American employees was mild compared to the fate of an executive in Caracas.

Trip to Venezuela

One of Stanford's most successful Latin American businesses was in Venezuela, where the CD sales were substantial. In 2006, he fired the president of the Venezuelan bank, a man named Gonzalo Tirado.

Stanford accused him of stealing money — a claim that may or may not have been true. Tirado questioned what was being done with the funds from the CDs and suggested that the company was engaged in fraud.

Stanford needed Tirado to shut up. If the man kept going on about a Ponzi scheme, the bad publicity would spread and cause South American investors, the backbone of the business, to flee.

The way he dealt with this threat is a dramatically revealing instance of Stanford's political influence and how he used it to protect his scheme. His connection with Caribbean Caucus member Gregory Meeks went back to the junket he financed in 2003.

Meeks represented a district in Queens, New York, with a large Caribbean population. In addition to being on the committee for financial services, he was on the House Foreign Affairs Committee and the Subcommittee on the Western Hemisphere. These "meshed nicely with Stanford's legislative interests," as a complaint later put it.[53]

In fact the Congressman was ideally placed to provide the particular favor that Stanford requested of him. He asked Meeks to push Venezuelan President Hugo Chavez to do a criminal investigation of the recalcitrant former bank president. They talked on the phone and Meeks said he would carry the message.[54] A month later, Meeks traveled to Venezuela to meet President Chavez and other officials.

To the Venezuelan government, Meeks was an important ally who might influence foreign affairs decisions in US Congress. Being on the left of the political spectrum, he was ideologically closer to Chavez than other American politicians.

His trip to Venezuela was ostensibly to thank Chavez for a program that provided affordable heating oil to needy Americans in the Northeastern states. Of course, Stanford's request was not part of the official agenda.

The Venezuelan government investigated Tirado. Later he was arrested for tax evasion and swindling. It is impossible to tell whether the charges had merit.

What is clear is that the investigation and arrest were a boon to Stanford. Tirado's credibility was ruined by allegations of criminal behavior; his claim that Stanford committed fraud became less believable — and hence less damaging.

Early that year Meeks and his wife went to Montego Bay, Jamaica, where they stayed at the Ritz Carlton hotel. The Congressman took six trips to the Caribbean with Stanford picking up the bills.[55] However expensive the private jets and luxury accommodations, one suspects that Stanford received a very high return on his outlays. Just getting rid of the Tirado nuisance must have been worth untold millions of dollars in CD sales that would not have happened if the ex-bank president had been free to keep complaining in public.

Stanford did not forget the favors he received and always showed his appreciation. In 2008, he became the top individual contributor to Meeks' election campaign. He and his staff held a fundraiser in the Virgin Islands for Meeks.

At the time they were in the midst of dealing with a major SEC investigation and tax liens filed by the IRS, but fostering the relationship with a political ally was so important that Stanford put in the time and effort to raise money.

A False Sense of Security

In 2004 the SEC started yet another examination. By then the regulator had been examining the Houston business for seven years, during which the company's revenues multiplied four-fold. As of October 2004, the brokerage customers held about $1.5 billion in CDs, including $227 million invested by Americans.

Preuitt, recalling that previous examinations failed to spur action, worried that the new effort might also be a waste of energy and resources. But she gave it a try, convinced that this was the right thing to do. What looked like a fraud was just getting bigger, pulling in more money and drawing in an ever increasing number of people in the United States.

As before, the investigators faced a tough task. The details of the portfolio underpinning the CDs remained unknown. The Houston company continued to tell the SEC that it could not get more information from the Antigua bank as to how exactly the money from the CDs was invested. It offered excuses as to why it lacked this information. The excuses changed, but the lack of information remained constant.

Stanford had various ways to keep his business under wrap. The auditor of the bank was part of the blockade against inquiries. This was the same auditor Stanford had hired for the Montserrat bank, a small accounting firm founded by one Charles Hewlett, a resident of Antigua and Britain.

Hewlett may have advised Stanford about Antigua and helped with his move there. The accountant stayed with Stanford for decades as auditor first for Guardian International and then Stanford International Bank.

CAS Hewlett was a one-man operation. Hewlett divided his time between Antigua and London, where he had a small office. In 1990 the Montserrat government had found that Hewlett did not qualify as bank auditor and Stanford was using the audits to withhold detailed information.

The audited financials for the bank in Antigua were similarly superficial. As the Stanford business grew, the accountant was probably incapable of doing a proper audit even if he wanted to. By all evidence he never had that capability and by the 2000s he was in his seventies.

Stanford told Davis, "God led me to Hewlett." This notion of receiving divine aid to find just the right corrupt or incompetent auditor reflected Stanford's general confidence that the deity was on his side. But he did not rely on God or luck in ensuring Hewlett's loyalty.

The accountant was paid large fees beyond the usual, sometimes off the books. In retrospect, we know that the financials he rubberstamped were false. But even without knowing that, one had to wonder about Hewlett as the auditor of a fast-expanding global bank.

This thought occurred to the examiners who tackled Stanford in 2004. As part of the investigation, an SEC lawyer contacted the British government to check the auditor's record. Britain's financial regulator replied that they had no information on Hewlett, had never heard of the firm. It did not even have a website.

That the bank at the center of the web of companies with billions of dollars in assets had an unknown auditor was a bright red light, regardless of any other issue.

To persuade their enforcement colleagues to pursue the matter, the examiners conducted an extensive investigation for six months. The resulting report made the danger clear. The CDs looked like a fraud on the basis of what was known, leaving aside the unknown contents of the underlying portfolio.

The examiners wrote: "not only is there no specific information available, the information that is available is highly suggestive of a fraudulent offering which would be inherently unsuitable for any investor."

The report contained a long list of warning signs and cited numerous federal securities laws that appeared to be violated by the sale of the CDs. It concluded: "The staff is concerned that the offering of the (Stanford Investment Bank) CDs may in fact be a very large Ponzi scheme, designed and marketed … to lull investors into a false sense of security by their claims that the Stanford International Bank products are similar to traditional US bank CDs."

At a March 2005 meeting attended by other federal and state regulators, the examiners presented the findings to the enforcement staff. Barasch looked annoyed, according to Preuitt. He remained adamant that no action would be taken against Stanford.

Then and there, without further considering the new report, Barasch and another enforcement official told the presenting examiner that this "was not something they were interested in." It was clear that he was not about to change his mind. Later Barasch could not recollect the presentation and his reply.

Realizing that there was no hope of enforcement action against Stanford with Barasch in charge, Preuitt waited. She prepared a memo but did not submit it until after Barasch left the SEC in April 2005. With him out of the way, the examiners again referred the case to the enforcement division. They warned that Stanford International Bank was possibly engaging in either money laundering, a Ponzi scheme or both.

The new assistant director of enforcement agreed with the conclusions, "including the deduction that this almost certainly has to be fraudulent." By then "Everybody, everybody believed that this was probably a Ponzi scheme," a staffer recalled.

Yet the investigation was almost shut down again. Preuitt fought from April 2005 through November of that year to get her colleagues to pursue the matter.

The enforcement group was convinced that building a case against Stanford was too difficult and therefore better not attempted. Trying to get information from Antigua was too frustrating. Worse, all the work could for naught and bad for a regulator's career. The higher ups in the SEC bureaucracy wanted plenty of straightforward, slam-dunk cases. By contrast, this was complicated and novel.

Some SEC enforcement people were unwilling to go after a possible Ponzi scheme that was not yet collapsing — they believed it is almost impossible to get evidence as long as the investors in a scheme are happy. By this reasoning, a case can't be made until the fraudsters run out of money and no longer pay investors.

In fact some Stanford clients and employees had complained, but the SEC had not pursued those complaints.

Hustle Sheet

Stanford was a master marketer. He whipped up the sales force's enthusiasm and aggression in every possible way — creating a frenzy of competition among groups of brokers and financial advisers. Cricket or CDs, his approach was the same.

Employees were coached and given seminars on how to pitch the product. Not all believed what they were told, judging from departures and complaints, but most did. They were constantly reminded that they could make 30% more than they made elsewhere and win gifts such as expensive cars.

Every week Stanford publicized sales teams' CD sales in a scorecard called the "hustle sheet." Offices around the world competed to push the most product, with the winners receiving flattering praise as well as material rewards. Successful teams were called "Money Machine" and "Superstars" — the same name he gave his cricket team. Many of the offices performed no other function but selling CDs.

The Houston brokerage received a 3% referral fee from the bank upon each sale, of which 1% went to individual broker. Financial advisers were given an additional 1% "trailing" commission through the term of the CD.

By contrast, selling conventional bank CDs involves little or no hoopla and fees are modest. As a general rule, CDs do not make a lot of money, so there is not much to be made from selling them.

Thus evidence that this product differed from other CDs was directly observable in the way it was sold. SEC examiners thought that the high fees and the failure to disclose fees and sales contests to clients violated the rules.

Stanford's rebuttal was that the payments to brokers and advisers were referral fees, not commissions. The change of words did not address the question of how CDs could generate such big payments, whether called fees or commissions.

"Mr. Stanford liked to just misname things," Preuitt said later. "Because he called it a CD, didn't mean it was a CD. Because he called it a bank, didn't mean it was a bank." The one exception to Stanford's penchant to stick sham labels on things was the "hustle sheet". That really was what its name said it was.

With all the wordplay, questions remained as to what the CDs really were. Regulators mulled over this matter year after year. If the Stanford notes were not CDs akin to savings accounts but rather securities – bonds, as some of the brokers thought – then they had to be registered as securities and what happened to the proceeds properly explained.

But there are ways to escape this requirement. Regulation D exemption is used for selling investments like hedge funds without registering them as securities. The catch is that such products can be sold only to accredited investors who have a certain amount of liquid wealth and therefore the wherewithal to take more risk. And under the exemption, the sales had to be private— public solicitation or offering was prohibited.

Starting in 1998, the Houston broker-dealer filed with the SEC a series of Regulation D exemptions. Via the loophole, the Stanford organization sold the CDs to Americans looking for higher return, many for their retirement accounts. This was a fast-growing market for Stanford. The first Reg D exemption was for sales of $50 million; in 2004 the potential offering had grown to $1 billion and by 2007 to $2 billion.

In 2002 SEC examiners found that the brokerage violated the terms of the Reg D exemption. The public Stanford website provided all the information people needed to buy the CDs and hence was in effect a public solicitation for unregistered securities. When some small hedge fund does this, regulators usually stop it.

But with Stanford, SEC enforcement refused to take action, hence the situation continued. In 2005 the Stanford company even ran a TV advertising campaign, stressing how secure the CDs were.

Anyone looking at the marketing materials and listening to sales people would get the impression that the high yields came at absolutely no risk. The investments were liquid and diversified; the CDs could be redeemed with a few days' notice; the Stanford company was regulated by the SEC and NASD and its successor, FINRA; the bank carried insurance from Lloyd's of London. What was there to worry about?

One relevant fact never mentioned was the amount of the insurance. In 2007, Lloyd's was covering $100 million worth of CDs, which at the time came to less than 2% of the total the outstanding deposits.

All the while, the sales spread further afield in the United States and the product was pitched aggressively for individual retirement accounts. Stanford established yet another company, this one in Baton Rouge, Louisiana, to be the trustee or custodian for retirement accounts. The term custodian, like the term CD, reassured investors, as if their money was kept in secure custody.

In fact, Allen Stanford had all the access he wanted to their IRAs. The trust was under his complete control, like all the businesses that fed his relentless appetite for funds. Brokers started to hear about problems at the Baton Rouge trust.

While the bank in Antigua had a small staff, the Stanford offices in the US, Latin America and Europe employed thousands, mostly in sales. Brokers and advisers, encouraged by bonuses and gifts, worked to convince clients to move their IRAs and other retirement accounts to Stanford and invest some or even all of their savings in the CDs.

Other products were offered as well, including a portfolio of mutual funds. But selling CDs was more lucrative.

The sales pitches brought in a wide range of investors, from a schoolteacher in Pennsylvania to petrochemical workers in Louisiana, seeking better returns on their retirement savings without compromising safety. These people were not knowledgeable about investing. They were all drawn to the CDs' attractive double feature of high interest and security, not available elsewhere.

Preuitt and other examiners worried about more investors being sucked in, with the scheme "just growing rapidly, and there appeared to be no end in sight."

As she later said, they "really tried to find ways" to stop it. They made persistent efforts to get the SEC to start building a case. Preuitt argued that if the Fort Worth office could not do this, it should be taken to a higher level at the Commission and the decision made there as to what to do.

Doubts persisted in the bureaucracy. This case was just too difficult. After Barash left and the SEC enforcement staff agreed to deepen the investigation, it took almost another year to get a formal order and subpoena authority. Finally in October 26, 2006, two years after the most recent examination started, enforcement opened another inquiry.

It looked like Stanford was in trouble. The examiners led by Preuitt had succeeded in focusing attention on the strange CDs despite the unwillingness of the higher-ups at the regulator.

Probably Knows Everyone

Anyone who worked in a government bureau that ever investigated Stanford was almost sure to be hired by him. Should they wish, they could get a high position in his network of companies or a contract as an outside consultant or lawyer to do well-remunerated work for his empire.

Just about any ex-government employee could be of interest to Stanford. Even being at a public entity that might in the future become involved with some aspect of his business was enough of a recommendation.

He surrounded himself with former government officials — certainly financial regulators, but also people from other branches of law enforcement. Among these was a former special agent who had been in charge of the Drug Enforcement Administration's Miami office.

To face the SEC inquiry, Stanford decided to reinforce his defense with additional legal firepower. His investment adviser business employed a consultant who was previously a branch chief at the SEC Washington office for compliance and examinations. When Stanford indicated he wanted another attorney, this consultant recommended Spencer Barasch, who had joined a law firm in Dallas after he left the SEC.

Stanford sounds overjoyed. "This guy looks good and probably knows everyone at the Fort Worth office. Good job," he wrote in an email. The Stanford company counsel contacted the erstwhile enforcement officer.

SEC employees are banned from representing clients to the agency for a year after they leave — though they can advise clients without representing them. Separately, there is a lifetime restriction on former federal employees regarding matters they were involved with while in the government. Federal conflict-of-interest laws forbid ex-employees to communicate or appear before the staff of a federal agency or court in relation to cases they worked on in the government.

When Barasch received the invitation to join Stanford's legal team, he emailed an ethics counsel at the SEC to ask that he be cleared to work for the financier. In this email he did not mention his past involvement with Stanford as enforcement officer. Instead, he wrote: "I am not aware of any conflicts and I do not remember any matters pending on Stanford while I was at the Commission."

Later Barash told investigators he did not mention his participation in decisions regarding Stanford to the ethics officer because he "just didn't remember anything" about those matters.

However, his deep-seated forgetfulness did not help him in this instance, because other people at the SEC Fort Worth office vividly remembered the prominent role he played in repeatedly blocking action in the Stanford case. They relayed some of this information to the ethics officer, who informed Barash that he was not allowed to represent Stanford.

The officer recalled telling Barash that he was permanently barred from representing the man and his businesses.

This conflict-of-interest decision angered Stanford, who called it bullshit. It was not just that ethical-legal niceties did not register with him—he actively sought situations where he could benefit from a conflict of interest. The fact that Barash had been involved in decisions regarding the Houston brokerage made him an especially attractive attorney.

But since it was not to be, Stanford quickly got over his frustration. Having failed to get his first choice, he went to a law firm called Chadbourne & Parke for an alternative. A partner at this firm, a friend of the general counsel of Stanford companies, proposed to set up an offshore hedge fund investment vehicle for the company.

It so happened that another partner at the Chadbourne & Parke Washington office, Thomas Sjoblom, was just the right lawyer for Stanford in his troubles with newly aggressive US regulators. Sjoblom had been at the SEC for around 20 years, an assistant chief litigation counsel in the enforcement division for 12 of those years and for a time as a special assistant US attorney for the Justice Department.

Since leaving the government he had made a name as a high-powered defense attorney with well-known clients such as HealthSouth founder Richard Scrushy and controversial financier Martin Armstrong. Though he was a Washington fixture, Sjoblom knew people at the SEC Fort Worth office that was investigating Stanford.

The Stanford company counsel who talked with Sjoblom mentioned that Wayne Secore, another erstwhile SEC lawyer, also worked for them. Clearly Stanford wanted all the former SEC officials he could get in his quest to block the investigation. He hired Sjoblom in the summer of 2005 to represent both the brokerage and the bank.

Sjoblom travelled to Houston and Antigua to talk with Stanford's associates and employees. When he asked them how the bank invested clients' money, nobody could tell him beyond the general description given in marketing materials. One financial advisor told him that the bank was not a commercial bank and the CDs were just "called" CDs – but were in fact more like corporate bonds.[56]

This observation reveals the deception embedded in Stanford's scheme from the day he founded the bank in Montserrat. The CDs were not real CDs, they were much riskier debt instruments. The attorney apparently took this information in a stride.

In Antigua, Stanford showed Sjoblom his ambitious plans for new property development and introduced him to the architect. This was Stanford in his element, showing off the plans for a large resort complex. Sjoblom became aware that some of the investments were financed by the Stanford bank. Had he thought about it, he might have noticed that the bank's revenue came from CD sales, which were not meant to finance ambitious resort building. One wonders what he would have done had he still been on the other side of the regulatory fence.

Doubts about the CDs was spreading, making knowledgeable outsiders wary. A financial adviser who was being recruited for Stanford said he would not want to go to jail (for selling the CDs). Such statements were "hearsay" according to Sjoblom. The long-time SEC assistant chief litigator and Justice Department assistant US attorney does not appear to have worried about these and other complaints against his new client. The fact that regulators did not follow up provided an easy excuse: the complaints had to be without merit.

But the SEC was starting to flex its muscles. The Stanford companies' compliance officer was told that the CDs looked like a Ponzi scheme. There was a demand for the records showing how the money was invested; the Houston brokerage repeated that it had no access to those records.

At the time the SEC staff hoped that a US attaché in Antigua might pressure Leroy King, the supposed regulator of the bank, to provide information.[57] When Sjoblom met King, the latter mentioned a letter he received from the SEC asking for help in investigating the Stanford bank.[58] King had immediately passed the letter on to Stanford and drafted a response with his help.

King told US regulators that the Antiguan Financial Services Regulatory Commission had examined the Stanford bank and would have detected any Ponzi scheme. Obviously further inquiry was unwarranted. The allegations sounded like innuendo rather than fact, King suggested.

He was very interested in who told the SEC that Stanford stole money — probably so as to give the names to Stanford, who would do what he always did to ruin the careers and finances of the whistleblowers.

Later in 2006 the SEC sent another letter to Antigua asking for assistance with its investigation. Again King showed Stanford and Sjoblom the letter and, as instructed by them, told the SEC that the Antigua Commission had done an onsite examination of Stanford International Bank just five months ago and all was well.

In fact King promised his blood brother not to audit the bank's investment portfolio. He even replaced or reassigned employees of the Antiguan regulator who looked too closely at the Stanford bank.

While thus shielded from scrutiny, Stanford could claim that the bank was under the regulatory eye — the Antiguan Regulatory Commission's website said it examined all banks on the island to make sure of their solvency, quality of investments and accuracy of reported returns. King assured Sjoblom that he would not allow the SEC to get the bank's records unless the Antiguan regulator itself decided the Stanford bank was engaged in a crime. Thus King honored his oath of loyalty to Stanford and paid his friend back in kind.

Sjoblom probably came to know as much about the business as anybody in the company with the exception of Stanford himself and Davis. The upshot of the lawyer's fact-finding expeditions to Houston and Antigua was a defense strategy centered on aggressively jamming SEC demands for information. He argued that the CDs were beyond the regulator's remit for two reasons. One, the bank that issued them was outside the US. He informed the SEC that Stanford would like to cooperate but Antiguan confidentiality laws prevented him from revealing the bank's investment portfolio.

Two, the CDs were not securities under US law, in part because the bank had "extensive insurance to protect against risk of loss." Laura Pendergest told him the CDs paid a "guaranteed" rate of return, taking away all the risk that an investor in securities mutual funds would be exposed to. Likely she was repeating what she'd been told.

Sjoblom boldly asserted that Antiguan regulation of the bank was comprehensive. Because of this and the extra capital and insurance coverage the bank held, CD holders were "virtually guaranteed payment in full" in the event the bank became insolvent.

SEC examinations over the years repeatedly raised questions about marketing materials that made the Stanford CDs sound as safe as FDIC-insured American bank CDs. The lawyer assured his former colleagues that the Stanford CDs were indeed as safe as or even safer than money in a US bank. What they made of the massive letter containing these arguments is not documented. There was no direct reply.

Sjoblom, with his long experience among the top ranks of regulators, appears to have mounted a powerful defense and set back the inquiry. He was careful to not to disclose certain information. After he looked over a risk report prepared for the bank's insurer, Lloyd's of London, he decided not to send it to the SEC.

In 2006 the lawyer left Chadbourne to join the prestigious law firm Proskauer Rose. In a memo he wrote on that occasion, he described his letter to the SEC staff as having led to the investigation being reconsidered. Instead of proceeding with its own inquiry, the SEC was now inclined to refer the matter to FINRA for lesser regulatory issues.

Stanford was obviously satisfied with the legal help he was getting; he retained Sjoblom and his new employer Proskauer Rose as well as the previous firm Chadbourne.

He was perfectly happy to spend lavishly on attorneys, in particular those who had once been in the government. His network of former regulators was his defense against immediate legal threats, while the lobbyists and political allies would help keep the law as favorable to his interests as possible.

Cover Our Rears

The SEC sent a referral letter to NASD describing various problems at the Stanford broker-dealer. It looked like the CDs were securities under U.S. law and they were sold to the public. That meant that Stanford was illegally operating an unregistered mutual fund.

This particular issue did not depend on what the Antigua bank was doing with the money — even if the investments were perfectly in line with what customers were told, the CDs were securities masquerading as bank deposits and as such a fraud.

In 2006 NASD started its own investigation of the brokerage. Stanford, not taking chances, quickly added yet another ex-regulator to his defense. He hired a NASD veteran of almost 20 years and the head of the NASD Dallas office, Bernerd Young. As chief of regulatory compliance for the Houston company, Young's job was to make sure the brokerage was above-board, or at least appeared that way.

In April 2007, NASD decided that there was indeed a violation — the sales material did not comply with advertising rules for several reasons, including failure to present in a fair and balanced way the risks and potential benefits of the CDs. "It contained misleading, unfair and unbalanced information," the brokerage regulator said.

Given the potential seriousness of the charge, the fine was modest — only $10,000. Stanford paid this without admitting or denying the findings.

That was the first of four fines that NASD, renamed FINRA in 2007, was to impose on the Houston company. Some of the violations were minor — the broker-dealer paid another $10,000 for failing to report transactions in municipal bonds within 15 minutes after execution.

Altogether the fines over two years totaled $70,000, an almost comical amount considering the magnitude of the business. Even if the money involved had not been comparatively trivial, Stanford was always willing to spend his way out of regulatory difficulties.

Former NASD regulator Young helped develop a guide for promoting the CDs to Americans. Young went to Antigua several times and visited the Stanford bank. He and other executives examined the bank's reports and watched PowerPoint presentations about Antigua and its regulatory process.

The sales training manual they developed may have conformed to the letter of advertising rules, saving the brokerage from additional charges. But it was not an example of truth in advertising.

This manual touted the liquidity of the bank's assets and the extensive risk management used to protect investments. It claimed that the bank's comprehensive insurance program was superior to FDIC coverage for US banks. This was "probably the only offshore bank in the world with this type of coverage." Neither the risk management nor the insurance corresponded with reality.

Despite his success in warding off the imminent legal threat, Sjoblom was worried. If regulators considered the CDs securities, they could easily show that the brokerage was illegally selling unregistered securities.

Moreover, whether or not the CDs were securities, in marketing the products the financial advisers were not doing the required due diligence and did not know enough about the underlying investments to advise their clients. They could face severe penalties for selling the CDs to people for whom these investments were unsuitable. And they were liable to be sued once regulators took action.

The company headquartered in Houston and the US business could be shut down on these grounds alone, with no need for any further proof of illegality. When Sjoblom warned of the risk of "battles on a larger and wider scale" with regulators, his client asked for ways to "get around" the problem.

Stanford wanted one of his staff to "get down to Antigua and cover our rears with tons of due diligence paperwork." That is, they would create regulatory compliance evidence to back up the sale of CDs. But Sjoblom was of the opinion that piling up the paperwork would not solve the matter of selling unregistered securities.

Other governments were becoming concerned. The Eastern Caribbean Central Bank was troubled by Stanford's ownership of both the Bank of Antigua, a commercial bank, and Stanford International. The Caribbean Central Bank sent Leroy King a letter about this. As usual, Stanford's counsel drafted a reply for King, who expressed his gratitude.

In 2006, a former employee named Lawrence DeMaria sued Stanford in Florida. He contended that the US firm was not only operating a Ponzi scheme but also laundering money from the offshore bank and using it to finance the brokerage.

According to this account, the Houston-headquartered business had no profits of its own; the entire enterprise depended on the bank in Antigua, that is, revenue from selling CDs. Stanford promptly settled the lawsuit and no more was heard from Mr. DeMaria.

Sjoblom hindered the SEC enforcement inquiry that started after the departure of Barasch but he could not altogether derail it. In September 2006 Sjoblom learnt that the SEC was taking the matter to another level as a fraud investigation. He kept up his tactics.

During a call, he told an SEC officer who once again asked for documentation that they had "no basis" to request Stanford International Bank's investment portfolio. He had "personally gone through all operations" and "there was no fraud here."

By that time it was difficult to reassure the SEC staff, who had heard from financial advisors that Allen Stanford was likely using clients' money to finance his real estate projects in Antigua. The investigators told Sjoblom they suspected Stanford was running a Ponzi scheme.

The attorney suggested that he himself was well-equipped to recognize the "hallmarks" of fraud, having spent 15 years investigating for the SEC. On the basis of his review of the situation and personal visit to Stanford International Bank, he found it to be an "incredible institution."[59] He blamed the SEC for making wild accusations.

In fact the organization truly was incredible, and not just in the sense of the word Sjoblom used — he meant extraordinary, and it was indeed unusual. But far-fetched would have been a more accurate description.

Despite the increasingly evident complicity of Leroy King with Stanford, SEC investigators continued their attempt to get the bank's records from Antigua and even considered a visit to the island. Sjoblom wondered whether to "throw them a few crumbs" by providing some documents.

Stanford had shaken off regulators relatively easily in the past. In 2006 it was no longer easy and the lawyer suspected that it was going to get tougher. Meanwhile he looked for ways to strengthen his connection to Stanford and do more work for him. He invited Stanford to the Virginia Gold Cup to meet the Venezuelan ambassador and learn about business opportunities in Venezuela that Sjoblom could help organize.

But the Chavez government took issue with the Stanford company in Caracas. This firm had hired a former US government employee – in keeping with the common practice in the group – as head of security. The Venezuelans accused the security chief of being a CIA spy.

Two years later in October 2008, the chief military prosecutor ordered a raid on the Caracas company, to investigate whether three of the employees were spying on Venezuela for the US government. This may have been anti-American propaganda on the part of Chavez, who faced elections and accused the United Stated of meddling in Venezuelan politics.

Then again, if Stanford was an informer, it would make sense for him to employ spies to collect information in Latin America. He refused to say anything on reports of his CIA connection. And that agency, like the DEA, would not comment.

Frustrations of a Reputed Billionaire

Pesky as the SEC had become, Stanford believed it was possible to put an end to the investigation. What he needed was further "insider" help to fight it. And what better insider than the former enforcement chief of the office conducting the inquiry?

Stanford decided that he really wanted Barasch on his side and made another attempt to hire him, about a year after his first try was foiled by the SEC ethics office. He emailed his lieutenants: "The former SEC Dallas lawyer we spoke about in St Croix. Get him on board ASAP."

This time Barasch apparently reasoned that the one-year ban was over and hence he was free to join Stanford's legal team. He emailed back to the company counsel who contacted him: "Thanks for the call this morning — I look forward to the opportunity to be of service to Stanford going forward."

Barash in Dallas and Sjoblom in Washington teleconferenced to discuss strategy as to how to foil their former fellow regulators.

Barasch was reassuring about NASD. He revealed his view of that body's effectiveness, probably a common view at the SEC: "I suspect that the NASD will just go through the motions to satisfy the SEC," he wrote. He was right, NASD went through the motions.

He commented on the response Sjoblom had drafted : "As much as I would like to offer you some brilliant suggestions, and show off my wisdom, I have nothing of substance to add. I think the content of the response, and its tone, are excellent."

But Barasch made an effort to contribute in another way. He asked Sjoblom for the names of SEC staffers working on the inquiry and called an enforcement officer he knew. This was "behind the scenes" work, for which he billed Stanford $6,587.

Both participants in that phone call later drew a blank as to the specifics of what they spoke about. It appears to be contagious memory loss. However, the former colleague remembered that he questioned whether Barasch was allowed to work on the Stanford matter at all.

Once again Barasch tried to get permission from the SEC ethics office. In his view, he was subject only to a one-year ban, which was by then over, leaving him free to help out with Stanford's defense.

But the ethics officer had told him the first time that he was not allowed to work for Stanford on the fraud investigation because he had a permanent conflict of interest caused by his involvement in the matter while at the SEC. Barasch claimed to have forgotten this, like so many other things having to do with Stanford.

Further, he argued that he had no conflict of interest because he did not remember any of the Stanford decisions he had a hand in. For a second time, an ethics officer had to tell him "no."

In view of his insistent efforts to get permission, we can infer that Barasch had a strong desire to work for Stanford. One has to wonder when this idea first occurred to him. It is common for SEC lawyers to leave for private practice. When he talked with Secore back in the 1990s, Barasch might have thought of his own career prospects as he contemplated that Secore had been at the SEC but was now a lawyer for the company owned by Stanford.

•

It was no secret that the financier liked hiring former regulators and paid them well. He was also known as a vindictive man who did not take kindly to anyone who accused him of fraud. If the thought of working for Stanford came to Barasch while he was at the SEC, he would surely have realized that it was better to stay in the potential future client's good graces and not try to develop a fraud case against him.

The SEC Inspector General pointed out: "for seven years the SEC enforcement staff did not open an investigation into Stanford although every member of the staff that had examined Stanford believed the CDs were a Ponzi scheme. That failure was due in part to repeated decisions by Barasch to quash the matter."[60]

Barasch later said he did not have the sole authority to close any investigation. But he claimed to have forgotten most of what went on. As a long-time regulator and lawyer, he had to know that he was best off deleting all this from memory.

The help from former insiders was not enough to stop regulators but it did slow them down — and the bureaucracy was slow to begin with. In late 2006 the SEC subpoenaed employees at the Houston brokerage and demanded documents from other Stanford companies.

Sjoblom used delay tactics to gain time for document production and testimonies. He ordered that certain files not be turned over to regulators. One was an agreement between the Antigua bank and the Houston brokerage showing that the latter managed some private equity investments for the bank. This link between the offshore bank and the US brokerage would have justified the SEC having access to portfolio information.

What's more, the agreement revealed that some of the money from the supposedly easy-to-redeem CDs was in private equity, a long-term investment that can take a decade to be sold. This by itself suggested that the CDs were pushed under false auspices, which might have been reason enough to shut down the US-based business.

One line of action had been open to the SEC going back to 1998, when investigators noted that the financial advisors selling the CDs violated their fiduciary duty because they put their clients into investments they themselves did not understand. The Houston company's own repeated claim that it did not have specific information about the investment portfolio was proof. It was possible to hang them by their own we-don't-know petard.

No additional information was necessary to make this particular case and it did not appear to be that difficult. But the new enforcement chief who replaced Barash did not go that obvious route. Later media reports said that another government agency pressured the SEC to shelve the action in 2006 — presumably the DEA, to protect its spy.

Later a member of Congress demanded the name of the agency that told the SEC not to enforce laws meant to protect investors. But apparently there was no response.

Instead of using the solution they had on hand, SEC enforcers pursued subpoenas to get information. Stanford's attorneys continued to play for time. While they used every trick on the books to delay the investigation, Stanford took in another $2 billion from CD sales through 2007.

Regulators were not the only ones demanding information from Allen Stanford. The complexities of his private life caught up with him. His erstwhile girlfriend, the Englishwoman Louise Sage, filed a paternity suit. This was surprising because Stanford did not dispute that he was the father of the children.

After becoming aware of his other relationships and moving out of the faux castle with her two children, Sage received a generous allowance. But when she married someone else, Stanford objected and stopped providing the luxurious lifestyle she was accustomed to – including private jets to take the children around. Thereupon Sage sued and demanded that he reveal his sources of income, alleging he made more than the $5 million he claimed for tax purposes.

Stanford settled the case without revealing financial information. But another potential demand for his financials was in the making. His long-patient wife filed for divorce in November 2007 after more than three decades of marriage.

Stanford himself never tried to get a divorce, although he spent most of the marriage openly living with other women. It is easy to discern a reason for his avoidance of divorce court. A legal proceeding held the danger that he would be ordered to produce documents on his financial situation so as to determine how much was due to his long-time wife.

Giving anyone a true account of his assets was out of question, while a false account might be detected. Thus his business and tax shenanigans intersected with his love life. Even if he wanted to get hitched to someone else – perhaps he would have liked to marry Sage – ending his existing marriage was too risky.

Hence he made no attempt to change his marital status. The court ordered him to pay his wife $100,000 a month for support and he bought a $1.3-million condominium in Houston for his grown daughter from the marriage. The divorce stalled, probably because he did not want it to go ahead.

Meanwhile, he was often seen in the company of his latest girlfriend Andrea Stoelker, a former cocktail waitress almost 30 years his junior. She held positions in his empire, was president of an arm of Stanford Financial and head of Stanford 20/20, an organization created for his cricket interests. He appointed her a director of the *Antigua Sun*. She was called his fiancée, as if they were planning to marry.

The lawsuits by his wife and ex-girlfriend added to the pressure that built up from all quarters in the last years of his career. Even in Antigua he was challenged. The Antiguan Labor Party had finally lost control in 2004. The opposition won a general election by a landslide, the Bird dynasty's hold on the country ended and Baldwin Spencer, who described Stanford as a neo-colonialist, became prime minister.

Stanford still owned much of Antigua and remained the government's largest creditor. He and Spencer had to work together. Still, the new government was less inclined to cooperate with him. When a businesswoman accused him of trying to get her off the land her company occupied at the airport, the Spencer government sided with her.

The hotels, restaurants, etc. that Stanford built were rarely, if ever, full. High-paying visitors were scarce. The investments typically lost money. His solution was to build more, on the reasoning that to draw the wealthy, you need an extensive network of proper facilities.

His ambitious plans to construct luxury housing on pristine beaches ran into resistance. A few Antiguans were concerned about the impact of construction on the delicate ecosystems along the shore. Stanford claimed to be a friend of the environment; he said he was repairing a reef. Not everybody believed him. After he acquired a small island, guards shooed away people who came by boat to watch the marine life.

He wanted to develop an exclusive enclave for the ultra-rich, with its own airstrip, hangars and dock, on the empty island he owned. That would allow planes to land, passengers to go through customs and get on their yachts, all in private. He believed he would make billions of dollars and poured at least $10 million into the preliminaries of the project. But the administration refused to give permission.

Stanford complained about Antiguans' unwillingness to let him go ahead and made a video explaining why he had to build all the planned components to get the full beneficial effect. It was reported that after frustrating talks with Spencer, he was so angry he punched holes in the mahogany paneling of his yacht. From 2007 on, he and the prime minister were publicly sniping at each other.

Then came the real estate bust and financial crisis. Everything Stanford bet on was badly hit as tourism and housing both slumped. One of the largest property bubbles was in Florida. He had invested in Florida real estate – buying some properties near peak prices – and given loans for developments in that state. Prices plummeted; the value of his investments collapsed; borrowers defaulted on his loans.

Other ventures failed as well. His Caribbean Star Airlines steadily lost money and had to be subsidized, as did the two newspapers. The gym and restaurants were nearly empty much of the time.

If he thought about it, he might have noticed an eerie similarity to the1980s economic downturn in Texas, the failure of his sports club and the debts that drove him to bankruptcy. But then his father still had the insurance brokerage and they could buy distressed properties on the cheap.

Now he was the owner or of numerous distressed businesses and he needed gargantuan amounts of money to survive. The ghost of Lodis could not help.

Stanford Would Likely Crush Us

The worst from Allen's viewpoint was that CD sales started to dry up. Clients took their money out and not much came in. His sales model, after bringing him huge sums year after year, stopped working. Stanford International Bank's cash reserve dwindled even as all his businesses needed large capital infusions.

He put ever more intense pressure on the brokers and advisers to sell the CDs. But an increasing number of employees in the United States were uneasy about the way the companies were run. Not only the source of the return on the CDs was a mystery, there were complaints about other products as well.

One of these was a portfolio of mutual funds that never performed as promised, as clients pointed out. In fact the returns in the brokers' pitch books were hypothetical and in part not supported by any data.

Mark Tidwell, one of the employees Sjoblom interviewed in 2005 to understand the business, had been recruited to the Houston brokerage with the usual promises. In exchange for high pay and big bonuses, Tidwell and his business partner, Charles Rawl, signed the employment contract that tied them to the company for years — if they left before the time was up, they'd have to pay back a large sum.

Soon after they started, Rawl and Tidwell were baffled by goings on at the company. They accepted Stanford's explanation that his CDs paid more than CDs available from US banks because the underlying investments were made by the bank in Antigua, where there is no corporate income tax. It made sense that this would boost the return.

But there was no way to explain the complaints about the mutual fund program and strange problems at the Stanford Trust company. Rawl and Tidwell wanted to know more about the products they were recommending to clients but could get no information. This led to suspicions and eventually a desire not to be involved with Stanford, but it was clear that he would sue them if they left.

The two brokers tried to arrange a deal where they would voluntarily pay some amount in return for being released from the employment contract. But there was no bargaining, as Stanford had no interest in letting them go. They resigned anyway, in December 2007.

Consulted about this, the lawyer Sjoblom suggested there was no threat of exposure — he told the company counsel that Tidwell was "bound by confidentiality."

Stanford immediately sued Tidwell and Rawl. They asked NASD's successor, FINRA, for arbitration, complaining that the Stanford company was engaged in unethical and illegal business practices. Stanford retaliated by discrediting them as disgruntled ex-employees.

Tidwell and Rawl learned that they were going to lose the arbitration — which meant that they not only had to compensate Stanford for having violated the employment contract but also had to pay his legal expenses.

By then Stanford had a lot of experience ruining employees who suspected fraud, did not want to push the CDs or related products and talked about what was going on at the company. With regulators not inclined to intervene, he relentlessly went after whistleblowers.

As many as thirty former Stanford brokers had gone through a similar arbitration process. As we saw, Hazlett and Basagoitia lost in arbitration several years earlier. FINRA and NASD ruled in Stanford's favor in every single one of these cases.

All such ex-employees were forced to pay the company hundreds of thousands of dollars while Stanford executives spread the word that these were not good people to employ, destroying their new job possibilities. Often the broker had to leave the industry and find another line of work not affected by the smear campaign.

It is worth noting that during the many years that brokers went to NASD and FINRA to complain about the Stanford company and its murky CDs, a career regulator named Mary Schapiro held top positions at these organizations.

Schapiro became president of the NASD regulatory unit in 1996, NASD chair in 2006 and the chief officer of FINRA in 2007, when it was formed. Under Schapiro, the brokerage regulator persistently sided with Stanford against any broker or adviser who turned whistleblower.

CD buyers had no idea that as many as 30 employees had complained of fraud to FINRA or that the SEC investigated Stanford on and off since 1997 and its examiners were pretty sure he was running a scheme. None of the serious fraud allegations showed up in public SEC and FINRA databases that investors can check.

Until 2007, there was no sign that anything might be amiss at all. That year FINRA registered the $10,000 fine Stanford paid for using misleading marketing material, but this appeared to be a correctable problem.

To an outsider, it looked like there was no major issue, only minor ones. FINRA sided with Stanford in arbitration case after case and the SEC took no action against him. As a judge later commented on the FINRA arbitrations in favor of Stanford, this was "evidence tending to support the Stanford enterprises' veneer of legitimacy."[61]

Clients encountered that veneer as soon as they met representatives of the Stanford companies. These were brokers licensed by FINRA, they and the investment advisers were registered with the SEC; the business was under the supervision of two regulatory entities. And the brokers and advisers assured investors that the bank in Antigua was heavily regulated in that jurisdiction and the deposits were insured.

Simply knowing about the complaints of fraud would have prevented people from falling into the trap. That the regulators not only failed to stop the scheme but did not make public the fact there were persistent warnings of serious fraud created false reassurance.

Meanwhile, whistleblowers from inside the company were left to hang. Their attempts to get away from the mess and protect their clients met with ferocious resistance. Stanford could not let them be, because their charges were too dangerous for him. He damaged or destroyed their careers so that they would not be credible, all with the tacit cooperation of NASD-FINRA led by Schapiro.

"It is an understatement to say that the regulatory process failed us," said Rawl later. "After realizing Stanford would likely crush us in arbitration, we accelerated our efforts to ask other regulators and law enforcement for help."[62]

Tidwell and Rawl counter-sued Stanford and brought their complaints to the SEC, which of course had been getting similar warnings, including its own examiners' reports, for years, to no noticeable effect. Eventually the SEC took testimony and evidence from Tidwell and Rawl.

Not Madoff

By April 2008, there were new complaints and evidence that the investment returns claimed for the CDs were false. SEC staff referred the complaints and findings to the fraud section of the Department of Justice for prosecution. Thereupon the Justice Department asked that while it determined how to launch a criminal investigation, the SEC stop its own inquiry.[63]

It is amazing how long the FBI took in view of its history with Stanford. He had to be well known inside the Bureau, which had looked for money laundering and drug smuggling in his organization on-and-off for nearly two decades going back to Montserrat. Moreover, the Federal Reserve had referred a fraud complaint to the FBI years ago.

Even so, the Justice Department moved at a pace suggesting no hurry at all. Possibly the DEA or some other US agency still sheltered the fraudster.

Later that year the Federal Reserve Board entered the fray with its own investigation, focused on whether Stanford International Bank was operating unregistered bank offices in Miami, Houston, and San Antonio. In a subpoena the Federal Reserve demanded numerous documents, including communications between various Stanford entities, and directly subpoenaed Allen Stanford.

This had the predictable result: Stanford immediately sought contacts at the Fed and former employees of the central bank who he could hire. However, that part of the government was new to him and at short notice it was not possible to find insiders who might be of help.

As investigators closed in, he spent more money than ever on building his political powerbase. In January 2008 he created his own internal lobbying operation in addition to the outside lobbyists he retained. He took an office at a proper Washington address, had it outfitted with expensive furnishings and hired two well-seasoned political operatives to run it.

One was a former chief of staff to a Republican Congressman who had chaired the powerful House Ways and Means committee, where tax law is shaped. The other was a former Treasury official under President Clinton. They were both appointed senior vice president for government affairs at Stanford Financial Group. To manage journalists, Stanford hired a State Department official from the Clinton years. She came to be known for her doggedness in batting away inconvenient questions.[64]

That year Stanford poured $2.2 million into lobbying. He put on showy Washington events, hosting a conference on the global financial crisis, with Madeleine Albright and Paul Wolfowitz as keynote speakers. The proposed theme of the event was that the private sector needed to work with government. Presumably no irony was intended.

Stanford himself, like most commentators, blamed Wall Street for the crisis. While this was received wisdom, his criticism had an edge of rancor. Big American banks did not do business with him and probably were not nice. His anger showed every time he spoke of their treachery.

Attorney Sjoblom managed to delay the Federal Reserve investigation, arguing that the company needed time to produce documents. He questioned the Fed's jurisdiction over the Stanford offices on the ground that these performed no banking function.

Strictly speaking, the only real bank in the Stanford network was the old Bank of Antigua, which was insolvent when he bought it as part of his takeover of the islands' economy and possibly never made money. On that basis one could argue that the Federal Reserve had no jurisdiction over Stanford.

Then again, selling bogus CDs issued by a bogus bank might have come under the banking regulator's purview. In practice, the question was moot. Numerous government entities had been suspicious and investigated Stanford for so many years. But none had stopped him. By the time the Federal Reserve came into action, the end was nigh.

As for Allen's testifying, his lawyer claimed he was not involved in the day-to-day operations of the companies. This prepared the ground for Stanford to deny knowledge of any problems. He would repeatedly assert he was a hands-off chief and left his subordinates to run the business.

All evidence suggests the contrary—he absolutely ruled the roost, down to whether employees were wearing the company's golden eagle insignia pinned on their lapels just the way he liked.[65] According to Davis, Stanford was a "charismatic dictator" and everybody at the company in effect reported to him.[66]

In December 2008, a few days before the Madoff fraud hit the news, the Stanford companies' clearing firm, Pershing, stopped wiring money for brokerage clients to buy CDs. Stanford tried to patch up an alternative way of wiring money via an intermediary escrow account at the Bank of Houston. Without fresh inflows he was running out of funds and if the SEC investigation became known, the lifeblood would stop flowing.

"Any publicity will kill us," he told his lawyers. For sure, word of possible fraud would end the CD sales altogether.

Stanford was still brazen. He announced that his business was not affected by the Madoff collapse and had come out of the financial crisis relatively unscathed, indeed in better shape than Wall Street. There was a lot of cash and he was building 10,000 condos in Miami, which would make a huge amount of money.

He said he knew what he was doing, if he were president of the US, the country would not be in the mess it was in, it would be back on the road to prosperity. He was putting new capital into the bank, personally contributing enough to boost total capital to over $1 billion. Thus he assured financial advisers as he pushed them to sell more CDs.

The supposed capital infusions, publicized in marketing brochures, added up to $741 million. The question was where this money came from.

In a conversation with an executive of the company, Stanford said this was the cash he had saved for the island resort investment. To further encourage confidence in his financial state, he promised to make a large contribution to that executive's church. He never did.

On other occasions he gave different explanations of the source of the capital, saying he raised it from Libya's sovereign wealth fund.

He magically conjured up assets. The island he bought in Antigua with the intention of building on it the exclusive compound of residences for billionaires – the project he'd been pitching unsuccessfully – was owned by his bank. By then, his wife was suing for divorce and he did not want assets to be in his name. Buffeted by the crisis, he had the brilliant idea to transfer the land to himself and then transfer it back to the bank at a valuation many times over.

Originally the bank had paid $63.5 million for the real estate. After the flip, the value would be put at $3.2 billion. This gimmick not only more than covered the capital contribution Stanford claimed to make, it would also compensate for the monies he had taken over the years. At one fell swoop, he could erase from the bank's books the "loans" he had given himself.

When Madoff came out with his confession, Stanford's lawyers emphasized how different his business was. Sjoblom declared in a conversation with an SEC staffer that "this was not Madoff — this is a real bank, real investments with global portfolio managers, and real assets."

Later Stanford threatened to punch an ABC News anchor in the mouth for asking whether he ran a Ponzi scheme. He was joking – and perhaps inebriated – but he knew the Madoff scandal was a threat.

A public outcry started as word spread that the SEC had failed to stop Madoff. This posed an obvious risk for the government bureaucracies that were involved with Stanford in some way or another. Members of Congress might ask awkward questions and make life unpleasant for higher ups at various agencies. Why had they not taken action? Why had they let two immense schemes fester?

The SEC in particular was exposed and had reason to do something about Stanford rather than dawdle, once the Madoff affair erupted. It was better to stop Stanford at once and claim credit for doing so. The longer they allowed the scheme to go on, the worse their political risk.

The FBI's criminal investigation was still at a preliminary stage. But officials there must have been worried as well. Even if Stanford had been a valuable informer for the government, now he was a liability. The decision not to protect him must have come from the top.

Concerned about any delay – after not being concerned for more than a decade – SEC chiefs got the go-ahead from the Justice Department to proceed with civil charges. This time the subpoenas were enforced.

It is striking how quickly regulators found clear-cut and overwhelming evidence of fraud once they decided to act and had the approval of higher ups.

Las Vegas and Tripoli

Stanford's behavior became erratic as his life went out of control, though he remained confident in public appearances.[67] In the last year or so he did things that made no sense. He decided to move the company headquarters from Houston to St. Croix and spent millions preparing for the move. With some hoopla, he revealed his plan to build an eco-friendly business park for his headquarters. It did not happen.

The developments he hoped would revive his business and make a fortune were stalled, but he kept pushing them even as the crisis eroded his existing business. His irate arguments with recalcitrant Antiguan officials succeeded only in further antagonizing them, confirming Baldwin Spencer's complaint of Stanford's "haughty, arrogant, obnoxious behavior."

The booziness that he managed to keep under wrap for much of his life became noticeable — he drank heavily and lost control when other people were around. He snarled at his staff, possibly more than he had in the past.

He had the $10-million-plus castle outside Miami demolished. Some months later, he razed to the ground a mansion on his St. Croix estate as well, after lavishly renovating and staffing it. It is not clear why he had the houses knocked down and whether he tried to sell them first. Of course, 2008 was not a good time to unload expensive mansions. Likely the loss did not matter to him. He had much bigger problems.

It must have been some consolation that his West Indies "Superstars" beat England at cricket in 2008. His team won the $20 million prize he gave at the tournament in Antigua's Stanford stadium. But nothing else he did worked.

By the end of the year he was taking $1 million a day from the bank just to keep his companies operating. He had to know the end was near. On a couple of occasions he asked the manager of his St. Croix estate to fill empty barrels with bank records and other documents. Then he burnt the barrels.

That December he took all his children and "outside wives" on a spectacular Christmas holiday, for the first time combining his various families, who apparently got along fine. They all flew on private jets to a luxury resort in Napa Valley wine country. The vacation cost more than a quarter-of-a-million dollars.

Then he and his fiancée, Andrea, went to Las Vegas, where he did some serious gambling. That week in early January 2009 he lost and spent over $515,000 at the Bellagio.

Clearly he was a well-known big gambler, because the casino gave him credit. He was allowed to sign for $258,480 in gambling markers — personal debt instruments. Bellagio executives were unpleasantly surprised when his check bounced. They sued, but by then there was a queue of tens of thousands of people who wanted their money back from Allen Stanford.

Besides gambling, he and Andrea went on a shopping spree in Las Vegas to buy jewelry. It was one last hurrah by a man who liked taking risk and lived it up to the hilt no matter what the circumstances. But it also looks like an omen that he was running out of luck, in life as well as the casino.

Extravagance was his style, but perhaps there was more to it. The good times tied his families and fiancée more closely to him.

•

Relatives who are grateful for how nicely you treated them are more likely to visit after you're locked up. Stanford's immense generosity to his mistresses and children looks less sweet when one considers that it was in his self interest to buy their loyalty — he did this with employees and politicians, and it sounds like he did the same with relatives.

Then of course there is the fact that the money he threw around with such abandon was not his. It belonged to others, many of them retirees who had been bamboozled to put their savings into his CDs. He was spending and gambling away their provision for living expenses, condemning them to poverty.

From his point of view, any additional money he wasted did not matter, given that he had already wasted billions of dollars. If and when he were called to account, another million here and there would make no difference. So he might as well spend as lavishly as he liked. But every dollar he spent was another notch down for his victims.

Compare his profligacy to what happened to them and his behavior comes across as sociopathic. James Flynn, a Vietnam veteran suffering from congestive heart failure, thought he was providing a financially safe future for his wife when he invested in the CDs. With their retirement fund demolished by Stanford, the Flynns had to sell their belongings. Some retirees, left near destitute, had to go back to work.

Even as Stanford gambled and frittered away other people's savings, he appeared to have hope for extricating himself. If he had enough money, maybe he could buy his way out and salvage what was left of his empire. He tried every which way to raise capital. To the last, he kept on pushing the CD sales, putting on new contests for brokers.[68]

Someone suggested he ask his friends. "I'll go to the Libyans. They love me," he reportedly replied. A Libyan sovereign wealth fund had invested $140 million or more with Stanford. But by late 2008 the Libyans started to pull out and managed to get at least $52 million of their investment back.

Undeterred, Stanford had an idea for a new deal with the government of Muammar Ghaddafi. He decided to go to the country to pitch it in person, discussed the planned trip with some of his friends in Congress and informed the State Department—or perhaps whoever he reported to as informant.

During the eventful January 2009 he flew off to Tripoli and offered Mohamed Layas, head of Libya's sovereign wealth fund, a 7%-to-8% stake in his bank. Layas wisely declined.[69] Libya withdrew another $12 million shortly after the visit.

Stanford travelled to Zurich, probably looking for wealthy investors who might be willing to buy equity in his business. Nothing came of it. Still seeking a way out, probably through the political influence of his cronies, he went to Washington. He talked with his main lobbyist, Ben Barnes, and consulted a lawyer at Barnes' office.

There Are Real Bullets Out There

While Allen Stanford flew around the world seeking relief from his troubles, a financial analyst named Alex Dalmady from Venezuela was about to make any relief for Stanford less likely. At the request of a friend who had bought CDs, Dalmady checked out Stanford International Bank some time in late 2008.

Upon examining the financial statements and other material available online, Dalmady quickly noticed that the bank had a unique business model. It was not a commercial bank; it did not make loans and earn the difference between interest rates on loans versus deposits. Neither was it an investment bank; it did not engage in fee-generating businesses such as securities underwriting.

It was like an asset manager rather than a bank. Indeed, Stanford's marketers often described the product as similar to a mutual fund, but miraculously without the risk.

Dalmady noted that the reported returns from the bank's portfolio of stocks, bonds, hedge funds, metals and currencies were exceptional. Each portion of the portfolio showed incredible performance. Every year the portfolio did better than comparable investments. For instance, gains from hedge funds averaged 22% annually, outperforming other investors' hedge fund portfolios.

Even in 2008, when almost all investments lost money, the Stanford bank claimed that its portfolio gained 5% to 6%. These numbers were public, available online. But there was no information as to which set of hedge funds earned 22% a year or what stocks and bonds made money during the crisis.

Examining the bank's website, Dalmady observed several anomalies. The bank gave the names of its board of directors – a proper thing to do – but the director responsible for investments was an 85-year-old cattle rancher and used car dealer. (It later emerged that this key board member, an old friend of Stanford's father from Mexia, had a stroke in 2000 and was incapacitated during the last eight years that he was listed as the board member who oversaw investments.)

There were disturbing inconsistencies. The 2007 audited statement said the bank had more than 50,000 clients; the 2008 audited statement said 30,000 clients. What happened to the other 20,000? The auditor was a local firm run by a 72-year-old.

Dalmady was not sure whether the bank's private equity investments belonged to the same portfolio. These included stakes in a resort developer, a golf club maker, an auction house, a restaurant and some movies. The analyst thought these sounded like a rich man's toys rather than serious investments. (In fact private equity did not belong in the CD portfolio, given that customers were told their capital was in easily sellable assets, but a small amount might have been justified as part of the supposed diversified mix.)

In short, Dalmady discerned what the SEC examiners first noticed years earlier. The bank wasn't really a bank and its portfolio returns were literally unbelievable. Unlike the SEC, Dalmady published his findings in short order. In the January 2009 issue of a Venezuelan journal, *VenEconomy*, he suggested that Stanford International Bank walked like a duck and quaked like a duck — so it had to be a duck. This was a scam.

He provided a plausible explanation of why governments let Stanford be for so long. The CDs buyers were scattered across the world; no single country had a large concentration of them; each regulator saw Stanford as outside its jurisdiction. Dalmady's article caused a sensation in Caracas and several blogs picked up the topic. Accounts of his findings spread through the global media.

Stanford could have avoided the adverse publicity by not posting the bank's statements online; it was not legally required. With his usual boldness, he advertised the wonderful returns as a sales pitch for the CDs. His audacious pushing of fake performance worked for years; nobody expressed doubt in public. Then just as regulators closed in, the suspicions came to the fore in *VenEconomy* and elsewhere.

People around Allen Stanford were frightened. A friend and business associate sent him a dramatic email in February. As usual in the Stanford empire when trouble showed up, the sender pointed to the need to get influential personages on board ASAP. "(T)hings are starting to unravel quickly on our side in the Caribbean and Latin America…(w)e need to come up with a strategy to give preference to certain wires to people of influence in certain countries, if not we will see a run on the bank next week," the message said.

The correspondent was aware that he and others faced extreme danger. "There are real bullets out there with my name on," he wrote.

They Are Not That Smart

The SEC was still trying to get Leroy King to cooperate. When Davis flew to Antigua in the last week of January 2009, King asked if they were going to make it. Davis said he thought they were going to be OK. King was noticeably anxious. Perhaps Davis started to make contingency plans for himself, if he had not done so already.

Investigators armed with subpoenas converged on Stanford. To figure out what to do, he met his top brass at a private plane hangar in Miami airport. Stanford was not willing to subject himself to questioning and tried to get the bank's president, Juan Rodriguez-Tolentino, and Laura Pendergest to testify instead.

Sjoblom told regulators that Stanford and Davis didn't know much about the bank's investments and Pendergest and Tolentino were better witnesses. He convinced them to postpone questioning Stanford and Davis.

But the lawyer was uneasy. In early February he asked an associate to check the Sarbanes-Oxley Act for what attorneys are required to do when they suspect that their client is perpetrating securities fraud. He also checked whether Antiguan law really did bar the Stanford bank from revealing its portfolio. He had used this argument repeatedly to the SEC but now realized that there was no such prohibition. He had not inquired about it before and apparently neither had the SEC, which could have found out that the main argument for denying them the information was wrong.

Pendergest and Tolentino were scheduled to be questioned by the SEC in February. In an email Sjoblom told them that Tolentino would have to testify under oath that the bank and the CDs were "real" and the money was invested as described in the documents, that the client funds were safe and secure.

Pendergest would have to explain to the SEC her supervision of the bank's portfolio. In fact she knew little about most of the portfolio, despite holding the title of chief investment officer for years.

Davis and Stanford divided the portfolio into three parts. A small fraction was in money market funds. A second part was invested in stocks and bonds by outside managers, as customers were told. These were the supposedly low-risk, easy to sell investments that Pendergest was responsible for.

Those two portions were dwarfed by the "third tier" of investments. Allen Stanford personally took care of the third tier with the help of Davis, who moved the money to wherever Stanford wanted it to be and kept the books. Hence Davis knew where the money was going, while Stanford himself made the decisions.

By late 2008 to early 2009, the third tier accounted for 80% or more of the bank's portfolio. Pendergest had nothing to do with managing this but was aware that tier three contained real estate and private equity. When the analysts who worked with her asked about the rest of the portfolio, she told them that tier three was very profitable and in the process of being restructured. The analysts were discouraged from further inquiry.

To deal with questions from the SEC, Pendergest would "have to get up to speed on tier three," Sjoblom wrote. She had to prepare before she testified.

In a series of meetings in Miami, there was bad news all around. Pendergest reported that the value of the tier two assets she managed had declined dramatically in the past six months, from $850 million in June 2008 down to $350 million. While markets crashed in the crisis, this was a steeper loss than one would expect from the broad downward move in stocks and bonds.

That the supposedly safe investments lost more than markets at large confirms that neither Pendergest nor anyone else at the Stanford company knew how to pick outside managers. But that was a secondary issue. The losses in tier three were worse. The hole that started 20 years ago had grown so large, nothing else mattered.

Davis revealed that the properties in tier three were fast losing value. Then there were the so-called loans to Allen Stanford. The SEC had noticed these transfers to him way back, when the amount was much smaller. Over the years he had rolled over the loans and taken more as he needed money for his ventures and spending. By late 2008 he owed the bank $1.6 billion to $1.8 billion. Estimates of the exact amount he took varied—it might be closer to $2 billion.

Since the investments he made in his own name were failing as well as the ones owned by the bank, he could not pay back any of the money. There was talk of Antiguan real estate worth $3 billion, but that was the $63.5 million land that Stanford schemed to flip and transform into $3 billion on the books—perhaps with supernatural help.

He told executives that despite all the problems, the company still had $850 million more assets than liabilities. But at a separate smaller meeting, he admitted that the bank's assets and financial state had been misrepresented. Moreover, the claim that he had provided or raised extra capital for the bank was not correct. The Libyans had not come through. There was no new capital, contrary to what the investors were told.

Those attending the meeting were shocked. Someone started to cry. Sjoblom suggested they pray together.

Afterwards the lawyer went into the office of an executive and announced: "the party is over." He told the company's general counsel that earnings had not been calculated properly and the assets may or may not be there. Sjoblom informed Davis and Stanford that they could face criminal charges, offering to represent them for a retainer of $2 million each.

Taking in the information, Tolentino realized that the bank was insolvent. He decided not to testify to the SEC, probably recognizing the danger of bearing false witness. Pendergest proved more amenable to persuasion and agreed to go before the regulators.

Her testimony was scheduled for February 10th. That morning Davis called her and told her to talk only about tier two investments. Thus he pushed her to mislead regulators — not a gallant thing to do, especially given their past romantic relationship.

 Sjoblom sat with Pendergest as she replied to questions as a sworn witness. She claimed "she was unaware of the assets and allocations of assets" in tier three, made no mention of the loans to Stanford and named only the lawyer as having helped her prepare to testify, not acknowledging that Davis and Stanford had been at the meetings.

Stanford kept up his confident front. He assured Davis that the SEC would not uncover anything because they were not that smart. Years of experience must have led to this low opinion.

But he was wrong. It was not the case that the SEC was incapable of finding out what was going on; the bureaucracy had lacked the will rather than the ability in the past. Once the higher ups decided to go ahead, regulators had little trouble getting all the evidence they needed.

Their quarry tried to gain time. Why he thought this would help is unclear. Did he still have hope of raising money? Did he think the real estate market would suddenly turn and bring up the value of his assets? Was he hoping for divine intervention in his favor?

Getting Pendergest to conceal key facts helped delay the endgame maybe by a few days. It certainly did not alleviate Stanford's problem. The immediate effect was to pit Pendergest, spinning a weak yarn, against government people who by then knew too much to be deceived and could only be annoyed by this dim effort to mislead them.

One has to wonder why Pendergest agreed to do it. She might not have understood the full implications of what was going on, having made her way up in organization by doing and saying what she was told to by Davis. Her role was mainly to cheer on the CD sales force while acting as the investment figurehead.

It was certainly not financial acumen that got her the high-paying position. Her one notable investment decision was related to her marriage to a Mr. Holt, a former personal trainer. She put $2 million from the bank's portfolio into a hedge fund started by her husband.

However, she had to notice that Stanford and Davis would not testify to the SEC themselves. Being trotted out as witness in this situation resembled being chosen as sacrificial lamb. A couple of weeks after her testimony, she was arrested on a criminal charge for failing to testify truthfully to the SEC.

Pendergest denied any involvement in the fraud. Later, Davis said that in 2007 Stanford assured Pendergest she could trust him as to how the bank's assets were invested.

•

She may have been deluded that she was doing the right thing by following the directives of the lawyer sitting with her as she testified. But Sjoblom represented the Stanford companies and was angling for a multi-million dollar retainer to represent Stanford and Davis in the criminal case to come. Pendergest's interest was not the same as theirs.

Four days after accompanying Pendergest while she committed what looked like perjury, Sjoblom informed the SEC that he was no longer representing the Stanford entities. He went further and asked that his past statements about Stanford – from 2005 through mid-February 2009 – be disregarded.

This unusual step, known as a noisy withdrawal, is seen as a signal that the attorney believes his ex-client is engaged in fraud.

I Did Not Know

On February 17, 2009, the SEC produced a complaint against Stanford. It was close to 12 years since the examiner Preuitt took a look at the CD sales and urged that the matter be further investigated. The complaint said Stanford and Davis ran a massive Ponzi scheme, Leroy King and Laura Pendergest facilitated the fraud and two Stanford company accountants helped cook up false reports of the bank's returns and investments.

It took a while for the government to find Stanford. At some point he may or may not have tried to escape from the US — a news report said he tried to get on one of his private planes but could not pay for a pilot to fly him. His bank accounts and credit cards had been frozen by court order.

Agents waited for him as he drove up to the home of a relative. He politely accepted the papers and they left. The charges were civil only; the SEC has no authority to take criminal action and the Justice Department was still working on the case.

While he remained free, Stanford was no longer allowed to leave the country and was asked to surrender his passport. He and his fiancée Andrea lived in a rented apartment in Houston; Louisa Sage and her two children from Stanford lived in the same building. He continued to travel within America, went to Washington to meet contacts and to Miami to see girlfriends and children.

In March, he and Andrea flew to Las Vegas — their second gambling trip in three months. He said it was to celebrate his birthday, a gift from Andrea. One gets the sense that however much he loved the Caribbean, Las Vegas may have been his favorite spot. And gambling had to be one of his favorite activities. Fifty-nine years old and facing serious charges, he wanted to have another try at Lady Luck. But there was no credit from the casinos this time.

Pendergast may not have realized what she was doing as she fell into the trap laid by investigators but Davis certainly knew what was up. In April 2009, a little over two months after the civil complaint papers were served, Davis pleaded guilty to conspiracy to commit fraud and obstruct an SEC investigation. He faced up to 30 years in prison.

Probably he was ready when the time came. He told the government what he knew in exchange for a lenient sentence. With him, the prosecutors had an inside witness who could enlighten them about every financial gimmick going back to Montserrat.

His old friend tried to counter by claiming the higher ground. In an interview, Stanford said that if any crime had been committed, it had to be Davis' responsibility. "If bad things were happening, he never brought them to my attention," Stanford told a reporter. "He did his job and I stayed out of his hair." This became one of his defenses — that Davis took care of financial details while he himself was an absentee owner, the big picture guy who founded the business and acted as its pitchman without being involved in daily operations.

"Everything we invested in was real," he declared on CNBC. "Anything that wasn't correct, I did not know."

Asked whether he gave information to the US government about his clients in other parts of the world, he replied: "I have nothing to say on that." He was adamant on not saying anything when the interviewer pushed harder with questions about his suspected moonlighting as spy.

Stanford was an old hand in public relations. But he did not help himself by complaining on television that he had to live like a poor man because the government froze his assets — having lost his private planes, he now had to fly on commercial airlines. Surely not many viewers sympathized with him for having to bear this hardship. That he did not realize the blunder, did not think of the simple fact that very few people have private jets and most fly commercial, says much about his life and mindset.

Another whopper was his claim that he always lived frugally. After announcing this to ABC News, he must have remembered that certain facts about his lifestyle were public — after all, the government had impounded his six private jets and two yachts. Yes, I had planes and boats, he admitted.

Sounding a bit annoyed, he repeated: "but I lived frugally." Clearly he used word "frugal" to mean something different from its usual meaning. One could paraphrase a line from *Alice in Wonderland* — frugal meant exactly what Stanford wanted it to mean, like the words CD or bank.

In the same interview he suggested he was closer to the common man than to the rich. This was true in a special sense — he ripped off the life savings of common people as happily as he took money from the wealthy.

Perhaps too much alcohol blunted his reason. His lawyer said that the fraud charges made Stanford depressed and prone to self medicating with alcohol.[70] The boozing, while not new, must have worsened under the strain. According to his attorney, once he started taking pills for anxiety, he stopped the excessive drinking. But it is unlikely that a lifetime of heavy drinking would end that easily.

Davis had tales galore, complete with bizarre details. Government officials who suspected and watched for 20 years could now get their fill of the long history of what in fact was a criminal enterprise from the very start. They might have had a second major witness in Stanford's long-time auditor Hewlett, but the octogenarian died before he could be called to testify.

By June 2009, some 20 years after the first suspicion of money laundering arose, the US was finally ready to indict Stanford.

Included in the 14 criminal charges were the bald lies he told in the desperate final months. He had claimed to add hundreds of millions of dollars to the bank's capital in late 2008. He had announced that the company was stronger than ever in early 2009. He had boasted, to journalists and customers, that his business escaped the Madoff fraud as well as the subprime crisis that decimated Wall Street.

In fact it turned out that the tier two investments contained an allocation to a feeder fund that channeled the money to Madoff. A report of this loss had been delivered to Stanford before he bragged that his bank did not invest with Madoff. It is possible he never looked at the report, having no interest in that part of the portfolio and little if any understanding of financial investments. His thing was tier three.

In the scale of the total scheme, the amount that went to Madoff was tiny. But it was yet another discrepancy that suggested Stanford diverged from the truth even in minor matters.

One afternoon in June 2009, Federal agents driving black SUVs surrounded the house where he was holed up with Andrea. His lawyer at the time, Dick DeGuerin, who also represented political pal Tom DeLay, informed Stanford that he was going to be arrested.

Upon learning this, Stanford went to pick up his suit from the dry cleaner so as to be properly attired. He always liked to do things in a certain style, though it could not have mattered much to the agents who came to the door.

Post Mortem on a Scheme

Among the few true things Stanford told reporters was his admission that at heart he was a developer, not a financier.[71] When he talked about investing, he meant real estate — he described his plans to build expensive housing or a new hotel. To show people what he did, he brought in an architect and spread out blueprints. There is no indication that he followed financial markets, let alone that he had any informed perspective about investing in stocks or bonds.

In retrospect, this appears to be the key to the CDs. Stanford needed credit for property purchases, construction and related activities. But he could not get loans from the obvious source that developers go to, namely banks.

When he started buying Texas real estate, he was a bankrupt former gym operator with a reputation for drinking and wild behavior. Bankers who knew something about his past would not lend him money.

There was also the matter that his financial records did not inspire confidence and he was never willing to provide much information. Any banker would have demanded to know more about the business. Stanford needed a source of money he could tap without revealing what he was doing.

Had he openly announced that he wanted to borrow in order to finance property development, he might have found a few takers. But the customer pool would have been small. He might have attracted some drug lords, impervious to risk and looking for ways to channel their earnings into legit venues.

Notes that said "certificate of deposit" and were supposedly as safe as US savings accounts but paid higher rates could be sold to anyone, not just clients with laundering needs. Once the bank got going, he had the means to finance his ventures on a grand scale. The CDs allowed him to implement his visions of island paradise housing, luxury hotels and whatever else took his fancy.

The claim that the proceeds were invested in high-quality securities and bullion by reliable outside money managers had to be a pretense from the start. Allen Stanford showed no ability to judge asset managers and neither did his tiny circle of close associates, chosen for their unquestioning obedience to him, not financial ability. With no skill at picking portfolio managers, he had no way of getting the higher-than-average returns he promised.

But that was not how he expected to make money anyway. He wasn't a financier, though for convenience sake we call him that. He was a property speculator who had found a great ruse to raise money. His entire financial career was a daring sham.

Most people who end up running Ponzi schemes don't wake up one fine morning and decide they will start a con game; they slide into it step by step. Their investment program fails; they conceal the losses, hoping to make good later. When that does not happen, they keep up the illusion by paying old investors with money from new investors. But Stanford was an exception; he deliberately set up a fraud. It was not that he deceived just to cover up losses. Even had he made money, his scheme would have been deceptive.

He sold CDs under false auspices to finance highly risky ventures. That the proceeds were invested in high-quality, easy-to-sell securities that carried little or no hazard was the original lie. He made that claim at the outset. It predated the losses and sham returns. Then he compounded his lie that these were safe investments by stealing a huge chunk of the money.

The Ponzi aspect of taking from some investors and paying others was a mere consequence, the only way to keep up the con. His main game was diverting the money to uses its owners knew nothing about, and that was intentional from the beginning. He wanted to develop real estate.

When he claimed he did not run a Ponzi scheme because he invested in real assets, in a sense he was telling the truth. He invested largely in real estate. His scheme began and ended with property development. This violated every promise made to the investors. Instead of the "globally diversified portfolio" of "marketable securities" that made double-digit returns as claimed, their money was in difficult-to-sell properties concentrated in Florida and the West Indies.

And since Stanford himself was the manager, there was nobody to vet his projects or set limits on the risk he took. Many, possibly all, of the developments he built operated at a loss. His response was to attempt ever more ambitious projects. These were stalled by the mid-2000s, but he continued to throw away the investors' money in his wildly unsuccessful enterprises.

The hole that started in Montserrat kept expanding because of the funds Stanford took for himself, the losses on properties he sank money into and the high commissions he paid to people who sold the CDs. He stole money all the time to finance his lifestyle and ventures, not to mention political influence outlays.

He was very careful to make sure that secret did not get out. Davis was told not to say anything to his wife. An accountant who recorded Stanford's "loans" on a spreadsheet was told he'd lose his job if any information were to leak. The gaping hole did not stop Stanford from claiming to have immense amounts of assets — in 2008 he gave out that his network of companies managed or advised on more than $50 billion.

Once Stanford was charged, a Texas court appointed a receiver to oversee what remained, a lawyer named Ralph Janvey. The records showed $7.2 billion in outstanding CD balances as of February 2009, but $1.3 billion of that was fictitious interest, so the Stanford bank owed $5.9 billion in principal to its depositors.

The market value of the assets the receiver found was only $500 million. There were properties outside the United States, but those were taken over by governments or receivers appointed by courts in those countries. In effect, Stanford had spent, paid to his sales force, lost – largely in property ventures – or left to the mercy of numerous governments a total of nearly $5.4 billion.

This was the money that kept him afloat for decades and bought him the allegiance of politicians and ex-regulators. It was an extraordinary sum for one individual to fritter away.

Do They Play Golf Every Sunday?

As soon as the SEC lawsuit hit the news, Spencer Barasch once again contacted the Commission's ethics office and tried to get permission to represent Stanford. Later he explained why he tried a third time after being told twice that it was not allowed: "Every lawyer in Texas and beyond is going to get rich over this case. Okay? And I hated being on the sidelines."

But he was disappointed. The 2009 answer was the same as it had been in 2005 and 2006. He was further disappointed when the Justice Department started an investigation into his dealings with Stanford.[72]

Fittingly, this news story was reported around the same time as a study by the Project on Government Oversight, which found that 219 former SEC staffers had filed 789 statements indicating their intention to represent a client before the SEC from 2006 to 2010. The trip Barash took through the revolving door between regulator and regulated is the norm, not an exception.

What's striking is that the regulators who go through the irresistible door stay close by — their main role is to help their clients by using their knowledge of and connections to the regulator. Thus Stanford wanted so much to hire Barasch because, as he said at the time, "This guy looks good and probably knows everyone..."

In May 2011 a Subcommittee of the US Congress held a hearing on the Stanford affair. During the hearing, representatives asked questions about Barasch.[73]

A member of the Subcommittee wanted to know the connection between Barascch and Wayne Secore — the previous head of the SEC Fort Worth office who was Stanford's counsel at the time the Houston brokerage first appeared on the US regulators' radar.

"Did Secore and Barasch have a personal relationship? Do they play golf every Sunday?" asked the member of Congress. That highlighted the early investigation quashed by Barasch after he spoke with Secore, though he and Julie Preuitt had different memories of the conversation.

Barasch was not called to testify. There was no reply to the question as to how friendly he had been with Secore. Even if he had testified, there would be no way to know whether he saw Stanford in the light of a future client while making enforcement decisions at the SEC. He likely would not have remembered, judging from his testimony to investigators.

The Justice Department brought civil charges against Barasch for violating ethics rules by representing Stanford Group. He settled the charge, paying $50,000 and not admitting any wrongdoing, as usual in such settlements. The government did not make a criminal case and Barasch was free to continue working as a lawyer.

So it came about that in 2011 the chairman of the Congressional Subcommittee, Randy Neugebauer of Texas, asked the SEC head of enforcement: "Were you aware that Mr. Barasch had business before the Commission last Friday?" The SEC official said he did not know that. Without a criminal conviction, there was no bar to Barasch representing clients to the SEC as long as he had not worked on the matter while at the Commission.

A group of investors sued the SEC, citing "the negligence and misconduct" of its employees and in particular the refusal by Barasch to shut down the Stanford operation after it became a subject of concern starting in 1997. The plaintiffs argued that "the SEC, which has a mandate to protect the public interest, in this case had both the authority and the duty to put an end to this scheme."

They would not have lost their money, they said, "But for the negligent acts and omissions, misconduct, and breaches of duty by Spencer Barasch, a former SEC regional Enforcement Director, the negligent supervision of Barasch by his SEC supervisors, and other inexcusable acts of negligence by SEC employees..."[74]

Had the SEC been a private entity, it would surely have been liable to those charges. But as part of the federal government, the Commission is protected by the notion of sovereign immunity. For the lawsuit to get around this protection, the SEC has to have a statutory mandate to report its examiners findings.

In defense, the SEC claimed it had not concluded before 2009 that Stanford was running a Ponzi scheme. Hence it did not have to report the findings.

Of course, if there is a settlement, it is taxpayers who will bear the cost of compensating the victims of regulators' negligence and misconduct.

Other Stanford clients tried a different tack and sued the Antiguan government on the ground that it was a partner in Stanford's crime. This suit demanded $24 billion in damages.

In response Antigua pointed out that Stanford's downfall devastated the economy, causing losses, layoffs and damage to reputation as a place for financial business. The country was broke.

But the fact remained that individual Antiguan politicians and officials benefitted from the fraudster's largesse. Leroy King, for one, stayed in Antigua and fought not to be extradited to the US.

An immense amount of litigation on a variety of complaints followed the Stanford scheme. The law firm that hired Barasch, Andrews Kurth, was taken to court by one of its clients for malpractice and other professional negligence. The client, Walton, was not an investor with Stanford but the owner of Galleria Towers in Houston, where Stanford Financial had office space. In 2005 Stanford and Walton negotiated about this space, both sides represented by Andrews Kurth attorneys. When the deal fell through, Stanford sued and tied up the property in litigation, costing Walton millions of dollars.

According to Walton 's complaint, in 2005 Barasch told his new colleagues at the law firm that they should represent Stanford in the SEC inquiry, thereby making them aware of the possibility of a Ponzi scheme and other illegalities at Stanford Financial.[75] On the ground that the firm concealed this information and continued to depict the brokerage as a legitimate entity to its client in the office space negotiations, Walton sought damages of at least $10 million.

All in all, in the long term the Stanford affair was unfortunate for the former regulators caught up in it. Thomas Sjoblom, whose tireless work on behalf of the swindler helped put off the day of reckoning, faced a number of lawsuits.

The Justice Department investigated his advocacy of Stanford. He had to leave Proskauer Rose, the firm he worked for. The receiver for the Stanford assets sued Sjoblom and the two law firms that employed him, accusing them of legal malpractice and aiding and abetting the Ponzi scheme.

The receiver's complaint charged that "Sjoblom, with 20 years of experience as a high-level SEC enforcement lawyer, entered the scene and spent the next four years delaying and obstructing the SEC's investigation of Stanford by lying to the SEC, telling the SEC that he himself had checked Stanford out and that it was not a Ponzi scheme, advising Stanford to hide documents from the SEC..."

Among the accusations: Sjoblom falsely told the Federal Reserve Board that Allen Stanford was not involved in the day-to-day operations of the various Stanford entities.

Separately, three investors (a Mexican and two US citizens) started a lawsuit against Sjoblom and the law firms. They sought class action status to represent other Stanford investors and more than $7 billion in compensation and punitive damages. The main allegation, similar to the receiver's, was that Sjoblom aided and abetted the fraud.[76]

About a month after she was charged with lying to the SEC, Laura Pendergest filed a $20 million suit against Sjoblom and Proskauer Rose for legal malpractice and breach of fiduciary duty. When Sjoblom prepared her for the testimony, he apparently failed to make clear that he did not represent her.

During the meeting with the SEC, Sjoblom was asked whether he represented Pendergest and replied that he did insofar as she was an officer of a Stanford company. According to Pendergest, the lawyer never told her that he was not watching her interest and she should have her own attorney, who likely would have advised that her best course was not to testify.[77]

The SEC took administrative action against several Stanford company executives, among them former NASD regulator and Stanford chief compliance officer Bernerd Young. The sales force training manual Young worked on became evidence that he and others armed financial advisors with misleading information.

These are vivid examples of the human material that regulators are made of. By all evidence the former regulators pursued their immediate self interest to the point of ignoring legal and professional obligations. Young in effect helped CD sales people bamboozle customers. Barasch impeded the discovery of the fraud while he was inside the government. Outside the government, both he and Sjoblom sought only to get billable hours with Stanford, whose deep pockets were of course always open. Between the two of them, Barasch and Sjoblom gained years for Stanford.

During those years he conned billions of dollars from thousands of people, including American retirees who put their life savings into his CDs, and ruined the careers of brokers and advisers who did not go along with his scheme.

It was said about Robert Vesco that he hurt or corrupted everyone he had contact with. Stanford, too, was bad news all around.

In the aftermath, even firms and people with very limited connection to him found themselves in harm's way. Thus the insurance broker Willis Group and certain of its officers were sued for acting as middlemen in Stanford's purchase of directors-and-officers-liability insurance and a bankers' bond from Lloyds of London.

A Willis employee had issued letters saying that Stanford bought this insurance. A Stanford salesman used the letters to give some investors the impression the CDs were insured and hence safe. A group of Mexican, Venezuelan and Panamanian investors claimed that Willis "should have known" about the fraud. Lloyd's of London was sued as well.

From the former regulators who worked for him to the insurers who sold him a bankers' bond, everybody would have been better off avoiding Stanford like the bubonic plague. The consequences for his family and political allies make a separate story, which we will look at later.

Has she been promoted?

"Have we done anything to thank her?" asked a member of Congress during the May 2011 hearing. "Has she been promoted? She probably should be running the agency."

Presumably the representative was being sarcastic. Members of the Subcommittee already knew that Julie Preuitt had been demoted.[78] She was sidelined, isolated and ostracized in the SEC bureaucracy, no longer allowed to oversee examiners and left without real work.

The treatment of Preuitt, the examiner who repeatedly warned that the Stanford operation looked like a Ponzi scheme and pushed for action to stop him, reveals higher-level regulators' priorities.

Preuitt was the great exception to the abysmal failure of the government to end the fraud before it caused widespread damage. Her subsequent troubles show the regulatory mindset in action inside its own world. There is no better explanation of why and how Stanford succeeded for as a long as he did and no clearer display of regulators' continuing inability to deal with any major con game.

During the years Preuitt pushed and nagged enforcement officers to pursue Stanford, many told her: "Why don't you just drop it? This isn't going to fly." She said at the Congressional hearing: "I am a rather tenacious person and didn't drop it."

She must have annoyed those colleagues who preferred to focus on matters other than the difficult and unpleasant task of nabbing Allen Stanford. She kept pushing them in a direction they did not wish to go, having reason to believe that this was not the way to get ahead in the bureaucracy.

But the failures at the SEC, while real, have to be seen in context. It is unfair to blame the SEC alone. This bureaucracy acted not in isolation but within the larger political and administrative environment.

Stanford developed layers of protection for himself. The immediate cocoon around him was the many former government people he employed. He made sure to be defended and advised by law enforcement and regulation insiders — a defense that was difficult to overcome.

If he obtained protection by becoming an informant, that would be a potent addition to his cocoon. It would explain why the SEC did not proceed in 2006 when it easily could have — it may have been asked by another agency to let Stanford be. There is no question Stanford would have been delighted to get himself under the wing of an agency like the DEA. Spying would be piece of cake for him.

Then there were his lobbyists and many political contacts. Any regulator aware of Stanford's high-level friends had to realize that this was a dangerous man to take on. A notable aspect of the story is how all regulators treated him and his business as a hot potato, to be thrown to someone else, if not out of the window. The SEC threw it to the Texas securities authority, FINRA and the Federal Reserve. FINRA wasn't sure about taking it on. The Federal Reserve threw it to the FBI, which presumably shelved it.

Nobody wanted to deal with the complicated scheme and well-connected and protected perpetrator. The SEC was not the only regulator or agency that looked at Stanford and then carefully looked away.

Then again, had the financial overseer insisted on pursuing the swindler, other parts of the government would have probably left Allen Stanford to his fate. This is what they did after the Madoff debacle showed up.

But having to push against other agencies meant increased career risk for SEC officers. It added to the regulators' burden were they to try to stop the scheme. No surprise that they strongly preferred not to take on the challenge. Preuitt was an outlier in this environment.

SEC headquarters in Washington puts out a parade of press releases describing achievements, thereby keeping the agency in the public eye and the good graces of its political masters. What's needed for this is a steady stream of successful actions. Certain technical violations are easy to spot—like missing required filings. It is also easy to catch garden-variety, small-scale fraud, which tends to follow a known pattern. And it is much less risky to go after men who lack the resources or wits to surround themselves with influential politicos and knowledgeable former regulators.

Insider trading, which became the preferred way for the SEC to bring prominent cases after the Madoff and Stanford scandals, presents an opportunity to regulators. Insider trading involves people giving each other information, often on the phone, and trading on that information in public markets. Phones can be tapped and trades monitored.

Moreover, insider trading does not have obvious victims and is not a clear-cut crime. The old-fashioned version practiced by corporate insiders abusing their privileged status is well known, but the broader application by regulators to anyone who might give or get information is novel. Because of these characteristics, the perpetrators likely did not think of it as a serious crime; hence they did not try to cover up, which made them easy to catch.

Going after someone like Stanford is difficult on multiple counts. His scheme was unusual, his Antiguan protection impenetrable. He practiced and enforced deep secrecy. His high-powered American defense team was capable of dealing shrewdly with regulators who might be their former office mates. He had prominent allies. All this was reason to ignore him and seek easy-to-catch violations that look like a lot of achievement on paper.

"There is no question that during the early Stanford time frame, Fort Worth senior management firmly believed that the office's success was measured strictly by the number of cases filed each year," Preuitt told the Congressional Subcommittee.

In 2007, a new associate director was named to the Fort Worth examinations unit. Pursuing the race for greater numbers, this official pushed a novel method for examinations of broker-dealers—little half-day interviews instead of a thorough look. By doing limited examinations, the unit could do more of them.

Of course, a mini-interview would never reveal anything about a scheme such as Stanford's or Madoff's. But the sheer number of examinations done would look impressive, gaining kudos for the office.

Preuitt and another examiner objected to this. As she put it, it was the same shortsighted mentality that she had battled in the Stanford investigation. Senior managers did not want to hear her argument against their plan.

Preuitt's objections earned her a reprimand. Her colleague who objected received a reprimand on his record as well. Two months later Preuitt was removed from her position, left without supervisory status or even clearly assigned duties. Staffers were told off for associating with her—in effect she became a pariah. No one in the bureaucracy was willing to talk with her.

Eventually SEC headquarters put an end to the mini-examination plan. Preuitt remained in limbo, although her complaint about the plan, like her view of the Stanford operation, had been on the mark. She felt under pressure to resign.

In 2009 the SEC Inspector General investigated the way she and her colleague were sidelined for questioning the policy proposal. It was found that senior officials' retaliation against them for voicing opposition to proposals was improper.[79] The Inspector General recommended that the two senior managers responsible for the actions be disciplined. But they were not punished and one was even rewarded with executive committee responsibility at the national level.

Asked about Preuitt's situation at the Congressional hearing, a director at the SEC headquarters explained that the senior managers could not be disciplined. They had gone through the correct bureaucratic procedure, had consulted human resources and counsel. As for Preuitt, he said there was an effort to find new responsibilities for her. The idea was to have her report to someone in another SEC office, probably in Denver, but not to restore her previous position.

At the time of the Congressional hearing, Stanford's crimes and the enormity of regulators' failure to stop him was headline news and an attention-grabbing topic. One would expect top officials to respond by punishing those responsible for the failure, reward those who tried to catch him, in particular Preuitt, and encourage serious efforts to detect fraud.

That the bureaucracy chose to do the reverse, that nobody was disciplined for failing to go after Stanford while Preuitt was in effect punished, shows that the agency has not changed its ways despite vows to perform better. The message is not to push for difficult actions. Better to go along with easy investigations, go through the motions and not bring up anything that might cause trouble.

At the Congressional hearing, representatives expressed astonishment at the situation. One responded to officials' explanations: "I could not possibly have understood your answer correctly."

But members of Congress come and go, whereas a largely unionized bureaucracy like the SEC stays in place no matter how dysfunctional and useless it turns out to be. The bureaucrats played for time, they would wait and the scandal would fade from public memory.

An Attitude Failure

The human cost of Stanford's game, the suffering he caused, was outsized. Unlike Madoff, he targeted a wide range of investors. Thousands of blue collar and middle class retirees invested their nest eggs in the CDs.

They were left without enough money to cover living expenses or pay mortgage and property taxes. Some lost their houses. Others could not meet their medical expenses. A retired public school teacher and his wife were both diagnosed with cancer as they confronted the disappearance of their savings into the Stanford black hole. A retired oil worker had to go back to work on an offshore rig.

Most of these people had been sucked into the swindle since 2005, when regulators had enough on Stanford to force him to shut down his CD sales in the US. The SEC could have closed the company for the advisers' failure to conduct due diligence about the portfolio, based on their own admission that they knew little about the investments.

Even if Stanford had successfully contested the action in court, the lawsuit would have served as a warning to investors. CD buyers would have taken out their money while there were more assets. This would have also acted as a warning to people in other countries.

"But instead of going forward … and immediately taking an action, they spent more time investigating and doing research and didn't actually bring an action until many years later," said the SEC Inspector General.

Members of Congress asked why the brokerage self-regulator, NASD and later FINRA, never did anything serious about the fraud allegations. By then Mary Schapiro no longer headed that organization; President Barack Obama appointed her the chairman of the SEC in January 2009. The promotion suggested that there was no major problem with her oversight of the brokerage regulator.

Since she now presided over the SEC, Schapiro did not have to field questions as to why NASD and FINRA sided with Stanford against whistleblowers who complained of fraud. Her successor had to deal with that issue at the Congressional hearing.

The FINRA Dallas office had stopped a 2005 investigation on the ground that the CDs from the offshore bank were not securities and hence not regulated under US securities laws. After the fact, the new FINRA chief recognized the superficiality of this mindset. "We, as well as the SEC, became overly intimidated by the jurisdictional issues and the issues as to whether the CDs were securities and didn't focus on the fundamental exposure and risk to investors," he said.

In hindsight, the quibbles as to what exactly the CDs were sound comical. They were not US bank CDs, therefore banking regulations did not apply. FINRA decided they were not securities, therefore securities laws did not apply — though the SEC decided they were securities. Apparently they belonged to a category all their own. Because they did not properly fit the pigeon holes regulatory bureaucracies go by, no regulator would take action. Or perhaps this was a useful excuse not to go after a man who for a long time seemed to be untouchable.

Allen Stanford has to be considered a genius among conmen. He concocted a way of tricking people out of their money while getting regulators to engage in endless theoretical arguments about the nature of his product.

The Stanford CDs were arguably a kind of IOU, a private debt instrument. But that is a mere technicality. In plain language, he peddled the means of deception and theft. As such, the CDs had to be illegal regardless of how exactly they were classified. For purposes of deception and theft, they were a very successful novelty, befuddling regulators year after year. In the innovativeness of his approach to fraud, Stanford beat any recent charlatan, including Madoff.

In 2010 the Dodd-Frank Act brought about an immense growth of government intervention in financial matters. Its promoters attributed regulatory failures to lack of resources and legal authority, hence the new law provided regulators with more resources and vast new powers. At the Congressional hearing on Stanford, testifying officials were asked whether Dodd-Frank would have made a difference. They all replied that it would have had no effect.

It was not the case that the ground-level investigators missed the evidence of fraud. On the contrary, SEC examiners quickly decided that the CDs were likely a scheme. No action was taken because of decisions made by higher officials.

"I do believe that they certainly were aware of the possibility of a Ponzi scheme back since 1997, and they had the manpower to be able to bring an action to attempt to stop the alleged Ponzi scheme from going forward," said the SEC Inspector General. "So I don't think that this was a question of lack of resources, no."

Neither was there a lack of legal powers. The head of FINRA stated: "This wasn't about rules and regulations. We had the rules and regulations on our books."

At the hearing, a chart graphed the numerous warnings and complaints over the years against the growth of the CD balances. Representative Neugebauer pointed out one major difference from the Madoff case: warnings of fraud started early, almost from the very beginning, when the amount of money was small. Had regulators done their job, they could have prevented the scheme. But they didn't, and more staff or additional regulations would not have helped. Senior officials deliberately decided not to take action.

Asked to identify the source of the failure, the SEC Inspector General answered: "It was an attitude failure." He mainly blamed the obsession with bringing more cases. "If you brought a case like Stanford, which was complicated and complex, involved Antigua, foreign issues, the question of whether the CD was a security, etc., that wouldn't give you a number very quickly. It would take a long time," he said.

That attitude does not seem to have changed. Under Schapiro, the SEC again boasts of its record number of enforcement actions, presumably to spiff up its image. Despite an internal restructuring, the attitude of the bureaucracy is the same, with Schapiro recycled from FINRA to the SEC.

So the larger budgets and staffs and extra powers Dodd-Frank brings make no difference as far as serious fraud is concerned. The next time regulators confront a thug of Stanford's caliber and wide-reaching influence, they will likely waste years again on abstract questions such as the exact meaning of the word "security".

Cell 505

Photos of Madoff walking to the courthouse in Manhattan, accosted by journalists on the way, show that the judicial system is willing to let alleged fraudsters remain free on bail while they stand trial. Stanford must have thought that he, too, would be allowed to post bail. But he was an exception in this, as well as in other ways.

The government considered him a serious flight risk. For one thing, it emerged that he had other passports in addition to the US passport he turned in when he was ordered not to leave the country. There were two Antiguan passports. One of these, a diplomatic passport, was in a briefcase government agents took when they seized Stanford's belongings. It would have been unusable anyway because it had expired.

His regular Antiguan passport was current. He had left it in Antigua but a friend brought it back to America for him. When he eventually turned it in, he said he had not mentioned it earlier because he was asked only about his US passport. But one would suspect that a man who had three passports and declared only one might have a fourth that he somehow neglected to mention, tucked away somewhere.

His lawyers argued that he lacked the means to escape, given that he no longer had access to planes, boats, credit cards or bank accounts. Then again, there turned out to be a Swiss bank account used by Stanford and Davis, from which $100 million was recently withdrawn. Stanford replied that this was not a secret account and the money had gone to pay back loans from the bank. There was still $20 million in the account.

If he had funds stashed away, he could have used his foreign connections to spirit himself to a country that does not extradite to the United States — as Vesco and other moneyed fugitives have.

Stanford claimed that his contacts would not help him escape. "While he has many prominent and influential friends in government and private enterprise all over the world, all occupy responsible positions and are law abiding," stated his motion to be allowed to post bail while the criminal case went to court.[80] But it would be no surprise if a few of his friends were a tad shady.

To show how much he travelled, prosecutors produced a spreadsheet listing the trips he took from December 2003 to February 2009. The list was 42 pages long and contained 2,127 entries. In these five years Stanford had constantly travelled around the world, never staying long in any one place. He had gone to 31 countries, among them Columbia, Singapore and Malaysia, presumably seeking to sell his CDs to unsuspecting inhabitants.

Furthermore, the government considered his travels while he was under investigation to be unusual and suspicious. There was the trip from St Croix to Tripoli and from there to Zurich. Stanford provided a statement from Andrea, saying that she went with him to Libya, that this was planned months earlier and cancelled due to schedule conflicts.

By this version of the events, Libyan officials were interested in developing the country's tourism industry as well as investing a large portion of their cash reserves with Stanford. So Allen and Andrea went there, met people and visited museums and cultural sites. The account has a surreal quality. He was not known for an interest in museums and cultural sites.

To make the case that he was no flight risk, he described Houston as his prime residence since 1985. But Miami was also a prime residence for years – the now demolished castle was locally famous – and St Croix too, since he designated the Virgin Islands as his residence for US tax purposes. Nevertheless, to show that he had strong ties to Houston, he pointed out that his various girlfriends and children were in the city as well as his wife, who lived there. Louisa Sage had moved from Dallas. His son from another woman was moving to Houston to finish high school in the city.

The moves showed "how committed the family is to fighting this battle together" as the memo put it. The unusually broad definition of family to include multiple girlfriends gave the impression of a man not inclined to go by the rules.

Prosecutors dug out records of Stanford's arrests. He had been arrested not once but three times before his final comeuppance. At the bail hearing, when he was supposed to come clean about his past, he failed to acknowledge the three prior arrests. These had not resulted in prison terms, but one does not get a sense that this is a law abiding citizen.

None of the arguments persuaded the judge that the accused would not flee. Stanford was not allowed to post bail. At the end of June 2009 he was sent to the private Joe Corley Detention Facility in Conroe, north of Houston.

It must have been an unspeakable shock. Here was a man who spent millions of dollars just to replace the teak panels of his yacht with mahogany, teak not being classy enough for him. He had spent years flying across the globe and sailing the West Indies. One can imagine his horror at being locked up with as many as 14 other prisoners in a cell with no window.

After decades of climbing marble stairways, walking on oriental rugs and sitting on tufted leather coaches, he had to get used to a dirty concrete floor and painted metal bunk beds. The bathroom was all steel and open. In the front of the room there was a TV set and to the side a small area with two phones hanging from the wall.

Stanford complained about the heat, the airlessness, the inadequate air conditioner in 100 degree weather. At times the power failed and the cell was left in total darkness. No doubt he was dreadfully uncomfortable. In August he complained of symptoms that sounded like possible heart trouble and was taken to a hospital for tests. By September he was back at the Conroe prison, despite efforts by his attorneys to get him transferred to a federal facility near their office in Houston.

In cell 505, he appears to have spent as much time as he could on the phone, probably with his girlfriends as well as lawyers. He hogged one of the two phones on the wall and his cellmates were forced to listen to endless conversations in his usual booming voice. They were increasingly annoyed, but he paid no heed. Perhaps he felt that as a man who played with billions of dollars, finagled numerous governments for 20 years and hobnobbed with top American statesmen, he wasn't about to kowtow to a bunch of low-life inmates.

On September 24, 2009, he was again on the phone, sitting in a chair facing the wall, his back to the other inmates. One of them told him he was on the phone too much and to get off. Stanford would not.

The man, identified in the subsequent investigation as white, yanked the chair backward; Stanford fell, the back of his head crashed into the concrete floor. The attacker proceeded to kick him, possibly other prisoners joined in.

By the time the guards got Stanford out of there and took him to the clinic, he was so badly beaten that his face was swollen almost beyond recognition. There was blood all over the phone area, the walls, the floor, the lavatory and one of the bunk beds.[81] Truly the place looked like a modern circle of hell.

As the medical personnel cleaned up his face, Stanford remained conscious and coherent. He was lucid enough to indicate that he was about to throw up and take the plastic tub offered. This happened repeatedly and he retched large amounts of blood into the tub. But asked his name, where he was and the date, he would not reply. He was bandaged up, handcuffed and taken by ambulance to a hospital.

These events are extensively documented in a video the prison administration made right after the incident as part of the investigation.

What happened afterwards is less clear. The broken bones in his face required surgery. His nose was badly broken, his cheekbone fractured and right eye damaged. His advocates pointed out that the government had locked up with brutal criminals a man who was not yet convicted and by law should be presumed innocent. A few days after the beating the judge granted the request to have him moved to a prison in downtown Houston.

Three weeks later he appeared in the courtroom, still spitting blood.[82] The judge stopped the proceeding to ask whether he was alright. Stanford refused a court officer's offer of help and, though gaunt and somewhat bruised, appeared to be in control of himself.

Initially his lawyer complained that he was put in a small cell and given no painkillers or antibiotics. But later other lawyers told the judge Stanford was given so many drugs for pain, anxiety and depression that he became addicted.

Stanford sued the Justice Department and FBI for violating his constitutional rights, demanding $7.2 billion. Among other charges, he accused the government of inflicting cruel and unusual punishment on him. A federal judge dismissed the case.

Delirium

He was no longer Sir Allen – Antigua revoked the knighthood – but a federal inmate with the registration number 35017-183. The man who owned yachts, planes, a castle and multiple estates was destitute. He once had a small army of former government functionaries to do his bidding, controlled an island nation, partied with US Congressmen and met the next President. Now he was kicked by fellow prisoners over the use of a phone.

Stanford rose as high and fell as low as just about anyone can in a modern society. So dramatic a downfall has to be disorienting, even without a beating on the head and a regimen of mind-altering prescription drugs.

Still he would not give up. He had pleaded not guilty to all the charges and vowed to fight every step of the way. That's what he did, initially using insurance coverage from Lloyd's to pay legal fees. As was his custom, he surrounded himself with expensive lawyers. But one after another lawyer resigned. He hired new ones. In the first year or so after his arrest, 10 attorneys came and went.

In less than a year, Lloyd's paid about $14 million for the defense of Stanford and his top collaborators. The fourth lawyer to head Stanford's defense, Robert Bennett, charged $1,000 an hour. At one point the well-known Harvard University law professor Alan Dershowitz joined the team.

But Lloyd's went to court and obtained a decision that Stanford had violated the contract by engaging in a form of money laundering. Losing the insurance coverage, he lost the pricey attorneys as well.

He could no longer pay his legal bills — or any other expenses. In 2010 he was officially declared indigent. The court appointed lawyers for him, a total of four, paid by – who else? – American taxpayers. This brought to 14 the number of attorneys who worked on the criminal case over several years.

Despite the beating he took, Stanford remained active in preparing his defense. He insisted that the government framed him and made him a scapegoat to ward off criticism of regulators' failure in the Madoff affair. He was innocent and his enterprise had been doing alright until the SEC took over and destroyed it. It must have been hard for the lawyers to try to substantiate this argument.

During most of 2010, Stanford met members of his defense team every day, including weekends.[83] The court provided not only for attorneys' fees but also the expenses of getting witnesses and documents. The government paid lawyers $150 an hour, not $1,000, but even so by the end of 2011 Stanford's defense had already cost taxpayers millions of dollars. Two companies that helped the lawyers prepare for the trial by searching for electronic evidence had been paid $1.7 million and billed for another $945,191, and that was just one portion of the expense of defending Stanford.

Nevertheless, he claimed that his defense was handicapped because of inadequate funds. As always in his life, he needed more money. In November 2011 he demanded from the court another $787,000 just to copy nearly 3,000 boxes of documents in the possession of the receiver—even though those documents were available for his lawyers to read at no expense. It looked like he wanted to spend taxpayers' money as freely as he used to spend his clients' money.

Judge David Hittner sought to bring some reality to the demands. "Stanford, as an indigent defendant, is entitled to a solid, capable, and competent defense, not the deluxe or "perfect" defense that he might have otherwise desired were he still in control of the millions (or even billions) of dollars indicative of his past lifestyle," the judge wrote. The spending was already massive and another million dollars could not be allocated to making copies of documents that were accessible in the original. That particular request was denied but Stanford cost taxpayers plenty in the years to come.

In a perverse twist, this St. Croix resident who schemed and lobbied tirelessly to reduce his contribution to the US tax till and owed hundreds of millions of dollars in back taxes was defended and kept at immense expense to people who did pay taxes. He stridently complained of not getting enough from the public trough, after having used every legal or illegal trick to avoid paying into it.

The law-abiding public, a body that he resolutely refused to join, had to finance not only his elaborate legal battles but also his expensive medical travails and even his phone calls— though that last may be limited by his cellmates.

The trial was put off for years. His lawyers argued that he was unable to assist in his own defense because he had become addicted to psychiatric drugs — although he had been meeting them daily in 2010. Three psychiatrists testified that he was not competent to stand trial; he suffered from delirium, either because of medications he took, brain injury from the beating or major depression.

In fact his substance abuse and psychological issues were of long standing. He was prone to extreme drunkenness and was taking anxiety pills before he went to prison — as his lawyer at the time told a judge when he was first arrested.[84] In combination with the beating and the drugs, his boozing over the years may have caught up with him.

Stanford was sent to a prison medical facility to be weaned off drugs. There ensued a lengthy rehab. After eight months in rehab and before the trial could resume, he announced that he did not remember anything that happened prior to his arrest in 2009.

Obviously he hoped that he would not be held responsible for events he professed not to recall. Maybe he got the idea from his erstwhile regulator and one-time lawyer, Barasch, who suffered from such wide-ranging forgetfulness with regard to the investigations at the SEC.

Stanford blamed the government for his memory loss. In emails to family members or friends, he wrote: "The government has fried my memory and my mind …I did literally lose my mind in October 2009 when I spent 23 days in a solitary coffin cell after suffering a severe concussion and recovering from major reconstructive surgery .." "I don't remember the good ol days or unfortunately anything else …"

But he claimed to have found God, as many do in prison. In the small cell he ended up in after the beating, he had been visited by the devil, a seductive presence according to his account: "God gave me the strength to see through Satan's beauty and his hypnotic voice and words to the core of his demonic being and the lying ..." he said in an email.

He himself was no novice in the lying department. But now he professed to be on the straight and narrow, with Mother Teresa as his hero: after "a long process of growing and healing and enduring pure hell in prison I was able to change to be a completely new and far better man to those I love and care for ..." He asked God for forgiveness for the way he treated his correspondent in the past.

However sincere his quest for spiritual improvement, Stanford's expressions of religiosity tend to have an opportunistic aspect. Whenever he invoked God, he was getting something tangible from the association. He quipped to Davis that God led him to the accountant who helped conceal the fraud. He told a group of his employees they should have three priorities in life: "God, family and me." They had to serve him as well as they served the other two priorities.

Back in 2002 the Wall Street Journal reported his tale of a Catholic priest he met in Antigua. The priest had wounds that Stanford described as the stigmata of Christ. He said he carried with him a vial of fluid drained from the priest's foot. This anecdote appeared in an article about Stanford's attempt to take from its owner the hotel property on gorgeous Half Moon Bay. He must have wanted to show his spiritual side to counter the image of extreme greed and corruption one gets from the article.

The priest with the stigmata was not heard from or mentioned again; he appears to have disappeared, though he became famous from Stanford's story. The colorful bit about the vial of fluid is still repeated in the media.

One Last Card

All accused persons would turn into spiritual amnesiacs if that were a way to escape prosecution. Neither the religious zeal nor the loss of memory helped Stanford legally. A prison doctor gave the opinion that he was just pretending not to remember.

By the time he was declared competent to stand trial, it was late 2011, nearly two-and-a-half years since his arrest. His last batch of attorneys wanted to resign like all the previous attorneys, but the judge would not let them.

Earlier on, Stanford's girlfriends and children sat in the courtroom to show their moral support. But in time they drifted away, facing their own problems. His mother, in her 80s, still showed up. And he had a new supporter. Notable among those attending the trial was an attractive young woman called Evelyn, a friend and paralegal who worked with Stanford's lawyers and helped with his defense.

She visited him in prison and testified that he could not recall past events. Writing in a blog she argued that the government made a catastrophic mistake, seized Stanford's belongings and destroyed his business without a case, and then tried to break him so as to make sure to get a conviction.

As guards brought him into the courtroom on the first day of the trial, Stanford looked like a caricature of a fallen con man. Dressed in an orange prison jumpsuit, no longer the flashy figure he used to cut in tailored suits, he sported a goofy grin. But apparently he had not lost his ability to charm, even from prison, judging by young Evelyn's emotional response to the verdict.

Davis, the prosecutors' star witness, testified for several days. The two long-time partners mostly ignored each other in the courtroom. Stanford's lead lawyer called Davis a "liar, hypocrite, adulterer, fraudster and coward" and portrayed him as the real perpetrator of the scheme. "The only company being investigated here was the company that Davis ran," the lawyer said.

Davis acknowledged that he lied, in part because he wanted to please Stanford. "I was proud. I was a coward. Later on I was greedy, regrettably," he admitted. But Stanford was the instigator; he had started the scam before hiring his college roommate, it was his creation. In the last day of his testimony, Davis pointed a shaky finger at Stanford and said if anyone wanted proof of the crimes he described, they just had to follow the money.

Stanford did not look at him. Neither did he testify.

Despite his part in falsifying the books and keeping up the pretense, Davis was a credible witness. While he ran the business operation, Stanford had full control of investments and took much of the money. Davis was paid well, making $14 million in salary over the years and additional bonuses and loans. Among his possessions sold off by the receiver were two BMWs, one of them a convertible, and a motorboat.

But what Davis made was piddling compared to Stanford's take of as much as $2 billion. The difference showed dramatically in their lifestyles. Davis lived like a successful executive but his boss lived like a exceptionally flamboyant billionaire. Why would Davis run a gargantuan scheme to pay for Stanford's ostentatious extravagance?

The jury believed Davis and convicted Stanford of 13 of the 14 counts, including money laundering, fraud and obstructing an SEC investigation. The one charge he was acquitted of concerned some Super Bowl tickets he bought for Leroy King.

Sentencing guidelines indicated a maximum of 230 years total time for the 13 counts. Evelyn shed tears, listening to the verdict. As he was led out of the courtroom, Stanford tried to reassure his friends. The show of bravado was not convincing.

Always the gambler, he played one last card. Until then he had refused to provide financial information, to give an accounting of the remaining assets or in any other way help his victims get back their money. He may have held on in the belief that this was a bargaining chip. Before the sentencing, he suggested that in exchange for a shorter prison term he would sign over assets in Antigua to the United States.

Funny that he suddenly remembered what he used to own — his amnesia appears to have abated. But those properties were no longer in his control; an Antiguan court took over and the government appointed local receivers.

Unlike Madoff, Stanford never acknowledged his guilt or any responsibility. He continued to play tricks through his trial. This was a pattern that went back decades. Stanford was far more aggressive and determined in his deceptions than Madoff, from the beginning to the end.

Though Madoff's overall scheme was larger, Stanford personally stole a lot more money. An interesting take on Madoff is that he did not take any of clients' funds for himself – he made money from his legitimate brokerage business – and deceived them because he could not face losing people's esteem by admitting failure.[85] Because Madoff simply took from some and gave to others, the money could be traced.

The trustee in the Madoff case recovered 65% or more of the invested principal, while the Stanford receiver may get back around 10%. That is a measure of the greater damage Stanford inflicted.

On top of it, he showed no compunction for his victims, only ridicule. "Stanford radiated contempt for others, particularly his depositors," the sentencing memo said. By all evidence that was a fair assessment. The prosecutor asked for the maximum 230 years for this "ruthless predator" while Stanford demanded a sentence close to time served, so he could get out of prison within months.

His victims had a chance to confront him at the sentencing. They were so numerous that they were asked to submit their names to a special lottery to pick those who would attend the hearing. Angela Shaw, whose family was ripped off by Stanford, spoke for the victims and asked them to stand up. They filled much of the courtroom.

Stanford, sitting at the front with his lawyers, never turned back to look at the victims.

He gave a rambling speech, blamed the government for ruining his legitimate business and attacked his bête noir, Wall Street. He claimed he that did not run a Ponzi scheme, he made investments that created synergies through companies that "supported, complemented and enhanced one another."

He meant the various tourist facilities he built in Antigua. But there was major synergy in his operation in another way — most of his companies were geared to selling fake CDs and channeling the proceeds for his use.

Not only had he no remorse, he did not even indicate awareness of what he had done. "If I live the rest of my life in prison, I will always be at peace with the way I conducted myself in business," he said. At one point he reminded the courtroom audience of his extensive political connections — he talked about going horseback riding with a former president. Indeed, the scale and reach of his crony network was remarkable.

His performance suggested that were he to get out of prison, he would do something similar again and hatch another scheme. Then he could use some of the money to buy the protection of regulators and politicians and go on to acquire new yachts, mansions, mistresses.

The judge chose not to impose the maximum sentence. Allen Stanford got 110 years. Though less than Madoff's 150, this was long enough to be described as a "Madoff sentence" of extreme length, doled out by courts to send the message that the government will punish financial villainy (if and when its functionaries decide to act).

You could say that the greater crook received the shorter sentence, one final instance of the long series of government failures concerning Madoff and Stanford. Of course, the difference in the sentences is purely symbolic, since neither man is expected to leave prison alive. Stanford was 62 when he was sentenced in June 2012.

For the rest of his existence he will almost certainly remain a ward of the Bureau of Prisons. He will serve only a fraction of the 110-year term before going to his last estate—as a pauper, after all the adventures and shenanigans, from bankrupt gym operator to billionaire financier Sir Allen and then to inmate 35017-183.

Fraudulent Transfers

An edifying intersection of the political and financial took place as the receiver of the estate tried to retrieve assets. Only a small portion of the funds could be recovered.[86] To make the victims' prospects worse, to try to get back money required so many lawsuits and litigation of such complexity that legal fees and expenses consumed much of the assets.

Stanford's profligacy was breathtaking; he gave not the slightest sign of prudence as he spent on estates, cricket, polo, casinos, girlfriends, pretentious offices, hand-outs to politicians and numerous other items. Selling his possessions typically brought in much less than what he paid. Thus he spent $21 million to buy and refurbish the two yachts, which sold for $1.4 million, less than 10% of the sum he spent. These, the tugboat plus the six planes he personally owned went for $8 million, a fraction of the cost.

Some of his belongings were strange—among the piles of items found in his offices and homes was a tapestry of Louis XIV of France, the "Sun King." There were numerous eagles in bronze or wood – many of them hideous – that would appeal only to people with a strong liking for decorative eagles. Much of this stuff sold as junk.

•

His investments had to be liquidated at immense losses. Much of the real estate located in America was in Florida, a place particularly hard hit by the slump. Properties that were acquired around the peak of the market had to be sold at a steep discount.

The private equity investments were badly chosen and timed. For instance, $40 million was in a small firm called Health Systems Solutions. In late 2008, Health Systems agreed to acquire another business and Stanford International Bank moved $9 million from CD inflows to an escrow account for the acquisition. But by then Stanford did not have sufficient funds to go through with the deal and it fell through. The other firm took the money in the escrow account.

Shortly thereafter, the SEC filed fraud charges. The receiver sued to get back the $9 million. Even if the lawsuit succeeds, the investment in Health Systems is an abysmal failure. The equity bought for $40 million sold for $700,000, telling evidence of lack of financial judgment in making the investment. Like most conmen, Stanford was a consummate salesman – with the "hustle sheet" his true symbol – but a horrible investor.

His victims faced an additional hardship. Like most of what they had been led to believe, the claim that the CDs were covered by SIPC was not true. Once the fraud emerged, they received an extra shock: SIPC refused to compensate them at all for their loss, on the ground that they did not lose money at a failed brokerage but on bank CDs. By contrast, Madoff investors quickly received SIPC funds.

In an unprecedented step, the SEC sided with the Stanford investors and sued SIPC, another government-created entity.

But the court agreed with SIPC that the purpose of its fund is to help the customers of failed brokerages, whereas Stanford investors were clients of the offshore bank even if they bought CDs through the Houston brokerage.

As is common in these situations, the receiver tried to get back bogus gains from Stanford clients who had redeemed their investments before the government took over. There is strong legal precedent for claw backs — thousands of victims of Ponzi schemes have been forced to return the profits they received, the Madoff case being the best known. Courts have persistently upheld the notion of getting back such payments, to be distributed to investors who did not redeem and lost their capital in the scheme.

It is a bitter surprise and hardship to investors that they have to return the gains they assumed to be theirs to spend. But in the Stanford case the more aggressive reaction came from the politicians and lobbyists who found themselves subject to similar claw backs.

What set Stanford apart from any old fraudster, his ability to acquire high-end protection and influence, depended on tainted money. His payments to American legislators and lobbyists, like the more overt bribes he paid Antiguans, came from the con game. The law regards all such payments as fraudulent transfers.

So the receiver Janvey set into motion a process to get the money back. He sent requests to the various political committees and individual politicians who received contributions from Stanford, Davis and their companies.

Some politicians voluntarily returned the money, among them Barney Frank and Christopher Dodd. The gargantuan financial regulation law of 2010 that carries their names is a symbol of these two political veterans' supposed opposition to financial shenanigans. Had they not returned the contributions they received from Stanford, the arch swindler, it would have looked unseemly even for Washington.

Gregory Meeks, who faced a complaint to Congress about his role as Stanford's message carrier to Hugo Chavez in the matter of the Venezuelan bank president, relinquished $6,600. But as of June 2012, less than $170,000 of the contributions to individual politicians had been returned; the receiver wanted back for the estate another $1.72 million. Most politicians were not forthcoming.

One excuse in these situations is that the money has already been given to charity — and hence cannot be returned. Representatives for Barack Obama, whose 2008 presidential campaign Stanford contributed to, said they donated it to charity. But legally, the recipient of fraudulent funds still has to return the money whether it is spent on philanthropy or for some other purpose, so that the original owners can recuperate some of their loss. Otherwise the retirees who were forced to return the profits on CDs could have also claimed that they donated for some good cause.

The large campaign donations that the receiver wanted to retrieve were held not by individual politicians but Congressional committees, both Democratic and Republican. All the committees ignored multiple requests that they return the money. After waiting for about a year, Janvey filed a lawsuit. In an unusual bipartisan accord, Democrats and Republicans together went to court to contest the case and keep the conman's dough.

Though the application in the political realm may have been novel, the receiver's action relied on the same well-established argument used to claw back phony profits from investors in Ponzi schemes. Like bogus investment gains, the political donations came from people who had been deceived out of their money.

In such cases the recipients do have one potentially valid defense. They are not subject to claw-back if they supplied something of value in return, that is, if the payment was for an "equivalent value" they provided. Thus Enron's fraud in falsifying its financial data did not mean everybody that did business the energy company had to return payments received. A pipe supplier, say, kept the money Enron paid for pipes because those added value to the estate. That value was a benefit to the creditors.

But the defense did not apply to the Democratic and Republican committees, or for that matter individual politicians and lobbyists. In refuting the objections, Judge David Godbey said the committees failed to show that they provided "reasonably equivalent value" for the money they received.

Of course, one could argue that politicians gave Stanford "value" for his donations; they provided him with some measure of protection of his interests and by associating with him bolstered his brand. If he really wasn't getting anything, he would not have given money. But that political return, being inherently corrupt, was not an argument in the favor of politicians and Congressional committees — the value provided to the fraudster was a loss to his victims.

For the investors, there was only harm from his political generosity, no benefit, equivalent or otherwise. His high-level political contacts made Stanford look reputable, enabled him to continue his scheme and defraud more people.

Politicians should not be exempt from the legal hardship inflicted on working-class retirees who had to return false gains even though they had little left to live on. The judge wrote: "Although as innocent beneficiaries of the Stanford Defendants' largesse the Political Committees deserve some sympathy in facing that prospect, they are not entitled to special treatment."[87]

Nonetheless, the political committees kept demanding special treatment. Both parties' committees appealed the court order.[88] Two years after the receiver asked for the return of the political contributions, only a small amount was back in the estate.

Lobbyists who worked for Stanford ran into similar legal trouble. The two he hired in 2008 for his internal lobbying operation faced lawsuits for the return of their salaries, bonuses and expenses — adding up to $525,000 for one and almost $400,000 for the other. The receiver sued the lobbyist Ben Barnes and his firm to retrieve more than $5 million in payments from Stanford over the years. He, too, fought the suit. Barnes did provide services to his long-time client, but as the receiver put it, those "had the unfortunate effect of attracting new victims to the Stanford parties' fraudulent investment scheme."

That could be said for almost all the government-related parties who came in contact with the swindler, from politicians and lobbyists to regulators—they all provided the wherewithal for his scheme. That the SEC and FINRA did not stop the game bolstered the impression that the CDs were valid. Former regulators used their inside knowledge and contacts to effectively shield Stanford. Politicians and lobbyists protected his interests and made him look good.

Political intervention created opportunity for special benefits to be carved out by the well-connected crook. Had Congress not tried to meddle with economic development in the US Virgin Islands, there would have been no ground for the special tax rate that benefited Stanford.

This explains his greater generosity to Democrats. Economic interventionism, whatever the rationale, allowed him more play. Democrats are more likely to back interventionist policies.

It was not that he favored left-liberal ideology. He did not promote general causes but rather specific benefits for himself. So when he mouthed platitudes about environmental woes, an issue associated with Democrats, he was pursuing his own particular agenda. He'd like to get subsidies for green energy or perhaps a tax break for the "eco-friendly" office park he was to build in St. Croix.

In response to this predator, government agents did what was good for themselves and their allies, to the detriment of ordinary citizens. Politicians went for campaign money and perks. Regulators took the bureaucratically expedient tack or looked to high-paying jobs on the other side. Those behaviors allowed Stanford to build and protect his empire.

•

The losers were not only his clients but also US taxpayers. The latter had to pay the taxes he escaped from and had to finance his defense and rehab and keep him for the rest of his life. While we are lucky that Stanford was toppled before he could use environmental gimmicks to steal even more from taxpayers, the money he took from investors was in effect largely tax-free for him. The IRS came up with a $432 million tab for unpaid taxes, but the receiver of the estate made clear he would fight any IRS attempt to collect from the meager assets left to the victims.

Like his lobbyists and political allies, Stanford's women were sued for the goodies he gave them. Gifts to mistresses, like campaign donations and lobbyist fees, originally came from the CD buyers. The efforts to reverse the fraudulent transfers from the scheme was resisted by many of the beneficiaries of the transfers. Ill-gotten though the money was, they claimed they did not have to return it. But they had no luck in court.

Girlfriends, his wife and his adult daughter were forced to relinquish the houses he bought for them. His fiancé Andrea had been paid a total of $560,000 by the company and the man personally. The receiver demanded this back for the estate.

So Stanford's lobbyists and political allies ended up in the same legal predicament as his mistresses — perhaps the one consequence of his scam that seems to be just.

SOURCES

Court Cases, Government Documents & Complaints

Janvey, Ralph S. v. Proskauer Rose, Chadbourne & Parke and Thomas V. Sjoblom. Case 1:12-cv-00155-CKK, last document accessed dated January 27, 2012.

Janvey, Ralph S. v. Democratic Senatorial Campaign Committee et.al. Case 3:10-cv-00346-N, last document accessed dated June 22, 2011.

Janvey, Ralph S. v. Ben Barnes and Ben Barnes Group. Case 3:10-cv-00527-P, last document accessed dated April 15, 2010.

National Legal and Policy Center, "Request for an Investigation into Activities of Rep. Gregory Meeks," letter to the Congressional Committee on Standards of Official Conduct, March 19, 2010.

Stanford Group Company Form ADV submitted to the US Securities and Exchange Commission, 2009.

Stanford Financial Group Receivership. "Political Contributions" last updated June 21, 2012.

Troice, Samuel et. al. v. Willis et. al. Case 3:09-cv-01274-N, last document accessed dated May 2, 2011.

United States House of Representatives Subcommittee on Oversight and Investigations of the Committee on Financial Services. Hearing on "The Stanford Ponzi Scheme," May 13, 2011.

United States Senate Committee on Banking, Housing and Urban Affairs. Hearing on "Oversight of the SEC Inspector General's Report on the 'Investigation of the SEC's Response to Concerns Regarding Robert Allen Stanford's Alleged Ponzi Scheme' and Improving SEC Performance," September 22, 2010.

United States Court of Appeals for the Fifth Circuit. United States, plaintiff, v. Robert Allen Stanford, August 24, 2009.

United States v. Robert Allen Stanford. Case 4:09-cr-00342, last document accessed dated June 6, 2012.

United States v. James M. Davis. "Plea Agreement" Case H-09-335, August 27, 2009.

US Securities and Exchange Commission Administrative Proceedings, last document accessed Aug. 31, 2012.

US Securities and Exchange Commission v. Stanford International Bank, Stanford Group Company, Stanford Capital Management, R. Allen Stanford, James m. Davis, Laura Pendergest-Holt, Gilberto Lopez, Mark Kuhrt and Leroy King. Case 3:09-cv-0298-N, last document accessed dated June 1, 2012.

US Securities and Exchange Commission Office of the Inspector General. "Investigation of the SEC's Response to Concerns Regarding Robert Allen Stanford's Alleged Ponzi Scheme," March 31, 2010.

US Securities and Exchange Commission Office of the Inspector General. "Investigation of Failure of the SEC to Uncover Bernard Madoff's Ponzi Scheme" Public Version, August 31, 2009.

US Securities and Exchange Commission Office of the Inspector General. "Investigation of Fort Worth Regional Office's Conduct of the Stanford Investigation," June 19, 2009.

Academic Publications

Akerlof, George and Paul Romer. "Looting: The Economic Underworld of Bankruptcy for Profit," *Brookings Papers on Economic Activity*, 1993, v. 24.

High, Jack. 1993. "Self-Interest and Responsive Regulation," *Critical Review*, v. 7, n. 2-2, Spring-Summer, pp. 181-192.

Kurdas, Chidem. 2009. "Does Regulation Prevent Fraud? The Case of Manhattan Hedge Fund," *The Independent Review*, Winter, v.13, n.3, pp. 325-343.

Newspaper and Magazine Articles, Interviews

Ackerman, Andrew. "SEC Loses Bid to Get SIPC to Pay Stanford Ponzi Claims," *WSJ online*, July 3, 2012.

Alderson, Andrew, Philip Sherwell and Patrick Sawer. "Sir Allen Stanford: how the small-town Texas boy evaded scrutiny to become a big-time fraudster," *The Telegraph*, Feb. 21, 2009.

Alexander, Paul. "On Cricket," *The Virgin Islands Daily News*, Nov. 2, 2006.

AliBaba staff. "Antigua Names New Regulator after Stanford Scandal," News.Alibaba.com, Sep. 1, 2009

Anonymous. "The Londoner's Diary: Allen Stanford's Final Chukka," *Evening Standard*, Feb. 20, 2009.

Baxter, Brian. "Andrews Kurth Sued for Malpractice Over Allen Stanford Work," *The AMLaw Daily*, April 14, 2011.

Barry, Rob, Michael Sallah and Gerardo Reyes. "Gregory Meeks' trip to Venezuela on behalf of Stanford's bank raises ethics questions," *Miami Herald*, Dec. 27 ,2009.

Bernard, Steven and Jeremy Lemer. "Stanford's Political Connections," *Financial Times*, February 20, 2009.

Berry, Scyld. "Stanford Was Made Bankrupt in Eighties," *The Sunday Telegraph*, February 22, 2009.

Bustillo, Miguel and Daniel Gilbert. "From a Small-Town Boyhood to Billionaire to Pariah," *WSJ Online*, March 6, 2012.

Blumenthal, Paul. "Convicted Congressman Tied to Arrested Businessman," Sunlight Foundation Website, Feb. 24, 2009.

Borland, Huw. "Tycoon Stanford Spits Up Blood In Court," *Sky News Online*, October 15, 2009.

Brumfield, Patsy R. "Stanford's Tangled Ties Spread Through, beyond Houston," *NEMS Daily Journal*, May 23, 2010.

Brush, Silla and Jim Snyder. "Stanford Maintained Big Washington Presence," *The Hill*, Feb. 17, 2009.

Bull, Andy. "Warning signs showed Stanford empire was built on threats and innuendos," *The Guardian*, February 19, 2009.

Calkins, Laurel Brubaker and Andrew Harris. "Stanford Officer Pendergest Holt Said to Have Plea Deal," *Bloomberg News*, June 19, 2012.

Calkins, Laurel Brubaker. "Stanford Receiver Loses Court Bid for Libyan Fund Freeze," *Bloomberg News*, June 13, 2012.

Calkins, Laurel Brubaker and Andrew Harris. "Stanford Financial's Davis Says Founder Conspired in Fraud," *Bloomberg News*, Feb. 3, 2012.

Calkins, Laurel Brubaker and Andrew Harris. "Stanford Judge Says Receiver May Need to End Search for 'Pot of Gold'" *Bloomberg News*, Oct 13, 2011.

Calkins, Laurel Brubaker and Andrew Harris. "Allen Stanford Loses Bid for $100 Million of Lloyd's Directors Insurance," *Bloomberg News*, Oct. 14, 2010.

Calvin, Michael. "Stanford's Proof That Money Can't Buy Class," *Sunday Mirror* Nov. 2, 2008.

Caribarena News. "Libya Rejects Stanford-Madoff Invite," February 25, 2011.

Churcher, Sharon. "The English 'Outside Wife' who Billionaire Stanford Jilted at the Altar...Twice," *Daily Mail*, March 15, 2009.

Churcher, Sharon and Simon Parry. "Revealed: The Secret of Sir Allen Stanford's Three 'Outside Wives'" *Daily Mail*, March 1, 2009.

Churcher, Sharon. "Palace Row over Cricket's Sir Allen Knighthood: Website's False Claim that Prince Edward Bestowed Honor on Stanford," *Mail on Sunday*, November 2, 2008.

Cohn, Scott "One On One With Stanford," interview on CNBC, April 20, 2009.

Connett, David and Stephen Foley. "The Stanford Files: FBI's First Probe Was 20 Years Ago," *The Independent*, February 22, 2009.

Dallen, Russ. "The Sir Allen Stanford Story: The Emperor Has No Clothes Revisited," *Latin American Herald Tribune*, Feb. 26, 2009.

Dalmady, Alex. "Stanford: Who Knew What When," Dalmady.Blogspot.com, February 18, 2009.

Dalmady, Alex. "Confessions of a Reluctant Whistleblower Or how the Blogosphere took on Stanford," *DevilsExcrement.com*, February 13, 2009.

Dalmady, Alex. "Duck Tales—Stanford International Bank," *VenEconomy Monthly*, January 2009.

Davis, Nick. "Allen Stanford: Antigua Feels the Fallout of Ponzi Case," *BBC News*, March 8, 2012.

Economist, The. "Allen Stanford. Arise and Fall," March 10, 2012.

Efrati, Amir. "The Stanford Affair: Another Bad Day for Proskauer's Tom Sjoblom," *Wall Street Journal Blogs*, August 27, 2009.

Elfrink, Tim. "The Fall of a Titan" *Miami New Times* April 09, 2009.

Fitzgerald, Alison. "Stanford Wielded Jets, Junkets and Cricket to Woo Clients," *Bloomberg News*, February 18, 2009.

Fleischman, Joan. "*The Miami Herald* Talk of Our Town column: King of the Castle Faces Paternity Suit," McClatchy-Tribune Business News, 10 June 2007.

Foley, Stephen. "Stanford's Lawyers Reveal His Depression and Alcohol Abuse," *The Independent*, June 26, 2009.

Forbes. "Allen Stanford," *Forbes 400 Richest List*, September 17, 2008.

Fowler, Tim. "Stanford Blames Regulators in Opening," *WSJ Online*, Jan. 25, 2012.

Fuller, Eli. "R. Allen Stanford in Antigua Hindsight," *Antigua Island Blog*, February 2009.

Gibson, Owen. "WikiLeaks cables: US suspected Allen Stanford long before ECB deal," *The Guardian*, December 20, 2010.

Gilbert, Daniel, and Tom Fowler. "Stanford Guilty in Ponzi Scheme," *WSJ Online*, March 6, 2012.

Gilbert, Daniel and Jean Eaglesham. "Stanford Sentenced to 110 Years in Prison for Ponzi Scheme," *WSJ Online,* June 14, 2012.

Goldstein, Matthew. "Stanford's Failed Health Club," Businessweek.com, February 13, 2009.

Gonzalez, Angel. "Prosecutor: Stanford Lied for Decades," *Wall Street Journal*, March 1, 2012.

Goodman, Alana. "Ben Barnes Sued for $5 million by Stanford Receiver," National Legal and Policy Center website, March 24, 2010.

Greenberg, Duncan. "Crazy for Cricket," *Forbes* suppl. Forbes 400, October 6, 2008.

Hans, Jennifer. "Ponzi Scheme is Money Laundering – No Directors And Officers Insurance Coverage for Robert Stanford Fraud," *LexisNexis* Communities Emerging Issues Law, Oct. 18, 2010.

Harris, Andrew. "Stanford Investors Accuse Lawyer, Law Firm of Aiding Fraud," *Bloomberg News*, August 29, 2009.

Hodgson, Andy. "Cricket's New Mogul Is Thriving on Adversity: Sir Allen Stanford and his family are used to making a profit when the going gets tough," *Evening Standard*, Oct. 28, 2008.

Houston's Clear Thinkers. "Is Allen Stanford Being Railroaded?" *Blog.kir.com*, July 9, 2009.

Ishmael, Stacy-Marie. "Sir Allen's Antigua, or the Curious Case of Stanford International Bank," *Financial Times Alphaville*, Feb 17, 2009.

Johnson, Martina. "Bird said He is Ready for Court Challenge to Electoral Law," *Antigua Observer*, December 19, 2011.

Koppenheffer, Matt. "The Massive Fraud Everyone Forgot About," *The Motley Fool*, July 6, 2012.

Kovach, Gretel C. "Stanford's Hometown Reels over Accusations," *International Herald Tribune*, Feb 21, 2009.

Krauss, Clifford. "Witness Says He Warned Stanford on Ponzi Plan," *New York Times*, February 3, 2012.

Lewis, Al. "Ex-SEC Attorney Saw Riches in Ponzi Defendant," and "Commentary: After Quashing Probe, Barasch Wanted to Cash In," *MarketWatch*, January 18, 2012.

Lichtblau, Eric. "Missing Texas Financier Located," *International Herald Tribune*, February 21, 2009.

McElhatton, Jim. "Both Parties Scheme for Ponzi cash," *The Washington Times,* July 26, 2011.

Meek, Andy. "After the Fall: The Messy Cleanup of Stanford Financial," *Memphis Daily News*, Sep 28, 2009.

Mendick, Robert and Robert Lea. "FBI Investigate Stanford over Money Laundering for Dangerous Mexican Drug Cartel as Cricketing Tycoon Goes Missing," *Daily Mail*, February 19, 2009.

Michaels, Dave. "Most Lawmakers Haven't Returned Donations from Disgraced Texas Banker Allen Stanford," *Dallas Morning News*, February 11, 2010.

Michaels, Dave. "Disgraced Texas Financier Allen Stanford Tapped Home Politicians as Allies," *Dallas Morning News*, Feb. 28, 2009.

Paton, Paul. "Who's Your Client?" *In-House Counsel*, Spring 2010.

Prince, Rosa. "Allen Stanford: From King of the Caribbean to Penniless in Prison," *The Telegraph*, June 9, 2012.

Protess, Ben. "SEC Official Demoted Despite Spotting Stanford," *The New York Times*, May 13, 2011.

Rosiak, Luke. "Texas Politico Rapidly Rises to No. 1 Overall Donor, Now No. 1 bundler," Sunlight Foundation Reporting Group, Jan. 6, 2010.

Ratcliffe, R. G. "Ben Barnes Reclaims Spot in Spotlight with Stanford," *Houston Chronicle*, March 10, 2009.

Rathbone, John Paul. "Money Laundering: Taken to the Cleaners," *Financial Times*, July 21-22, 2012.

Reilly, Ryan J. "Allen Stanford Drops Suit Against Feds For Allegedly Violating Constitutional Rights," *TPMMuckraker*, March 24, 2011.

Ross, Brian. "Allen Stanford's Tearful Interview," ABC News, April 6, 2009.

Roth, Zachary. "Stanford 'A Wreck Of A Man' As Defense Team Turns To Dershowitz," *TPMMuckraker*, May 19, 2010.

Roth, Zachary. "A Washington Tale: As Feds Closed In, Stanford Boosted Efforts To Buy Influence," *TPMMuckraker*, January 5, 2010.

Roth, Zachary. "Six Degrees Of Allen Stanford," *TPMmuckraker*, February 18, 2009.

Rothfeld, Michael. "Stanford Says He Has Lost Memory," *WSJ Online*, Sept. 15, 2011.

Rovzar, Chris. "Report: R. Allen Stanford Asked Representative Gregory Meeks to Get Help From Chavez," *New York Magazine*, Dec. 29, 2009.

Salant, Jonathan and John McCormick. "Democrats Have More Cash Than Republicans for Off-Year Election," *Bloomberg News*, February 1, 2010.

Sallah, Michael and Rob Barry. "As feds closed in, Allen Stanford Scrambled to Keep Fraud Secret, Money Flowing," *Palm Beach Post*, Dec. 6, 2009.

Sallah, Michael and Rob Barry. "Feds Probe Banker Allen Stanford's Ties to Congress," *Miami Herald*, Dec.21 ,2009.

Sawer, Patrick. "Cricket Tycoon Sir Allen Stanford Caught up in Spying Row," *The Telegraph*, Nov. 9, 2008.

Scannell, Kara. "Attorney to Settle in Stanford Ethics Case," *Financial Times*, January 14-15, 2012.

Scannell, Kara. "Top Lawyer's Withdrawal From Stanford Case Waves a Flag," *Wall Street Journal*, March 6, 2009.

Scherer, Ron and Brendan Conway "Investment Fraud Suspect Stanford Was Major Political Donor," *The Christian Science Monitor,* February 19, 2009.

Shaw, Beth. "Texas Billionaire R. Allen Stanford Hospitalized after Jail Fight," *RightJuris.com,* September 26, 2009.

Shields, Mitchell J. "R. Allen Stanford's Former Moneyman Points Finger at Former Boss," *New York Post,* Feb. 9, 2012.

Shields, Mitchell J. "Mud Flies in Stanford Trial," *New York Post,* Feb. 8, 2012.

Simpson, Glenn R. and T.W. Farnam. "Texas Businessman Sought Influence in Corridors of Capitol," *Wall Street Journal,* Feb. 18, 2009.

Smith, Greg. "Record show Rep. Gregory Meeks Took Six Caribbean Trips with Wife - on Tab of Con Artist," *Daily News,* Dec.28, 2009.

Staff Reporter of The Wall Street Journal. "Antigua, Island of Sun, Is Also in the Shadow of R. Allen Stanford — He Owns Sundry Enterprises, Lends to the Government; Will He Get the Half Moon?" *Wall Street Journal,* Mar 5, 2002.

Stecklow, Steve. "Hard Sell Drove Stanford's Rise and Fall," *Wall Street Journal,* April 3, 2009.

Steffy, Loren. "R. Allen Stanford doesn't face his many victims," *Houston Chronicle,* June 15, 2012.

Steffy, Loren. "Allen Stanford Sentenced to 110 Years in Prison," *Houston Chronicle Business Blog,* June 14, 2012.

Stoffel, Brian. "You're Wrong about Madoff, and that Ignorance Will Hurt You," *The Motley Fool*, April 27, 2012.

Swartz, Mimi. "The Dark Knight," *Texas Monthly*, May 2009.

Sweeney, John. "Stanford Drug Informer Role Claim," *BBC News*, May 9, 2009.

Tolson, Mike and Dane Schiller. "Before Scandal, Stanford Left Texas for World of Wealth," *Houston Chronicle*, February 21, 2009

Vincent, Isabel and Melissa Klein. "Hide and Meeks – Shady Charities, Odd Financial Disclosures, Love of Junkets Dog Queens Congressman," *New York Post*, March 21, 2010.

Weiss, Debra Cassens. "Stanford Investors Sue Proskauer, Chadbourne and Ex-Partner Sjoblom in Texas State Court," *ABA Journal - Law News Now*, Jan 5, 2012.

Whitehouse, Kaja . "Public Lawyer Named — Stanford's New Slap," *New York Post*, Sept. 16, 2009.

WikiLeaks. "US diplomats warned about Stanford," *The Times of India*, Dec. 22, 2010.

Wilonsky, Robert. "In Dallas Federal Court, Those Swindled by Allen Stanford Sue SEC For Failing to Stop Him," *Dallas Observer*, March 25, 2011.

Wyatt, Edward. "Ex Official at SEC Settles Case for $50,000," *The New York Times*, January 14, 2012.

Wyatt, Edward. "Former SEC Official Said to Be Subject of Criminal Inquiry," *The New York Times*, May 13, 2011.

Young, John. "Citizen Stanford and His Many Influential Friends," *Waco Tribune-Herald*, March 8, 2009.

Books

Coll, Steve. *Private Empire: Exxon Mobil and American Power*. The Penguin Press, 2012.

Frankel, Tamar. *The Ponzi Scheme Puzzle: A History and Analysis of Con Artists and Victims*. Oxford University Press, 2012.

Henriques, Diana. *The Wizard of Lies. Bernie Madoff and the Death of Trust*. Times Books, 2011.

Hoffman, Robert. *Sir Allen & Me: An Insider's Look at R. Allen Stanford and the Island of Antigua*, Southern Cross Publication, 2009.

Herzog, Arthur. *Vesco: From Wall Street to Castro's Cuba The Rise, Fall, and Exile of the King of White Collar Crime*, iUniverse, 2003.

MacKay, Charles. *Extraordinary Popular Delusions and the Madness of Crowds*. L.C. Page & Co. 1932 edition, original publication 1841.

Markopolos, Harry et al. *No One Would Listen*. Wiley,, 2011.

Redding, Eric and D'Eva. *Great Big Beautiful Doll*. Barricade Books, 2nd edition, 2007.

Springer, Kenneth S. and Joelle Scott. *Digging for Disclosure: Tactics for Protecting Your Firm's Assets From Swindlers, Scammers and Imposters*. FT Press, 2010.

NOTES

1 The notion was that Mississippi contained immense amounts gold and silver, which would back the notes issued. This was a delusion; nobody actually brought back treasure from Mississippi for this purpose.

2 As described in MacKay's Extraordinary Popular Delusions and the Madness of Crowds. It was not called an option but rather "fictitious" stock.

3 An image of this photograph and some of the Antigua Sun text that was published in the Wall Street Journal at least twice, including Simpson and Farnam, "Texas Businessman Sought Influence in Corridors of Capitol," February 18, 2009. It was also published in the Latin American Herald Tribune; Dallen "The Sir Allen Stanford Story: The Emperor Has No Clothes," Feb. 26, 2009.

4 In an interview with Forbes. Also quoted by Andy Bull in "Warning signs showed Stanford empire was built on threats and innuendos" The Guardian, 19 February 2009, and Tim Elfrink in "The Fall of a Titan," Miami New Times, April 09, 2009.

5 For an interpretation of this crisis, see George Akerlof and Paul Romer, "Looting: The Economic Underworld of Bankruptcy for Profit," Brookings Papers on Economic Activity, 1993, v. 24.

6 She grew up in Mexia, but was not born there.

7 That is, to the ambitious of the 16th century — Niccolo Machiavelli in The Prince, ch.7.

8 The high number is unlikely. It comes from "Warning signs showed Stanford empire was built on threats and innuendos" The Guardian, 19 February 2009.

9 Plea Agreement of James M. Davis, August 27, 2009.

10 The information comes from the court testimony of Davis in 2012.

11 See Scyld, "Stanford Was Made Bankrupt in Eighties," The Sunday Telegraph, February 22, 2009, p. 9. Also Sharon Churcher, "Palace row over cricket's Sir Allen knighthood: Website's false claim that Prince Edward bestowed honor on Stanford," Mail on Sunday, November 2, 2008.

12 Connett and Foley, "The Stanford Files: FBI's first probe was 20 years ago," The Independent, Feb. 22, 2009.

13 For convenience I will refer to the country as Antigua; the full name is Antigua and Barbuda.

14 See Herzog, Vesco: From Wall Street to Castro's Cuba.

15 Mentioned in Complaint by the receiver against the lawyer in Janvey v. Sjoblom.

16 Janvey v. Sjoblom.

17 "Antigua, Island of Sun, Is Also in the Shadow of R. Allen Stanford — He Owns Sundry Enterprises, Lends to the Government; Will He Get the Half Moon?" Wall Street Journal, March 5, 2002, and "Sir Allen's Antigua, or the curious case of Stanford International Bank," Financial Times Alphaville, Feb 17, 2009.

18 "Antigua, Island of Sun, Is Also in the Shadow of R. Allen Stanford — He Owns Sundry Enterprises, Lends to the Government; Will He Get the Half Moon?" Wall Street Journal, March 5, 2002.

19 Janvey v. Sjoblom.

20 Janvey v. Sjoblom.

21 "Warning signs showed Stanford empire was built on threats and innuendos" The Guardian, 19 February 2009.

22 US Securities and Exchange Commission Office of the Inspector General, "Investigation of the SEC's Response to Concerns Regarding Robert Allen Stanford's Alleged Ponzi Scheme," March 31, 2010.

23 Meek, "After the Fall: The messy cleanup of Stanford Financial," Memphis Daily News, Sep 28, 2009.

24 According to Davis, in his 2012 testimony.

25 According to testimony in 2012 by Joan Stack, human resources manager at Stanford Financial.

26 US Securities and Exchange Commission Office of the Inspector General, "Investigation of the SEC's Response to Concerns Regarding Robert Allen Stanford's Alleged Ponzi Scheme," March 31, 2010; p. 33.

27 Springer and Joelle Scott, Digging for Disclosure: Tactics for Protecting Your Firm's Assets From Swindlers, Scammers and Imposters. FT Press, December, 2010.

28 Connett and Foley, "The Stanford Files: FBI's first probe was 20 years ago," The Independent, Feb. 22, 2009.

29 Sweeney, "Stanford Drug Informer Role Claim," BBC News, May 9, 2009.

30 Later the SEC Inspector General found that the enforcement inquiry was likely opened because of the money laundering matter rather than the examiner reports warning of fraud.

31 US Securities and Exchange Commission Office of the Inspector General, "Investigation of the SEC's Response to Concerns Regarding Robert Allen Stanford's Alleged Ponzi Scheme," March 31, 2010.

32 Krauss, "Witness Says He Warned Stanford on Ponzi Plan," New York Times, February 3, 2012.

33 In 2012 Davis testified that Stanford used "money, flattery, intimidation and fear" to control people.

34 We don't know for sure how effective Stanford's influence was, but the fact remains that he got much of what he wanted on the issues that mattered to him, though not all.

35 Roth, "Six Degrees Of Allen Stanford," TPMmuckraker, February 18, 2009.

36 Blumenthal, "Convicted Congressman Tied to Arrested Businessman," Sunlight Foundation, Feb. 24, 2009.

37 Sallah and Barry, "Feds probe financier Allen Stanford's links to lawmakers," December 28, 2009.

38 Ratcliffe, "Ben Barnes reclaims spot in spotlight with Stanford," Houston Chronicle, March 10, 2009.

39 Steve Coll Exxon Mobil and American Power. The Penguin Press.

40 Stanford Financial Group Receiver's political contributions list.

41 Simpson and Farnam, "Texas Businessman Sought Influence in Corridors of Capitol," Wall Street Journal, February 18, 2009.

42 Ralph Janvey "Receiver's Original Complaint against Ben Barnes and Ben Barnes Group LP," US District Court, at the Northern District of Texas, Dallas Division, March 15, 2010.

43 Glenn R. Simpson and T.W. Farnam "Texas Businessman Sought Influence in Corridors of Capitol," Wall Street Journal, February 18, 2009.

44 Subcommittee on Oversight and Investigations of the Committee on Financial Services of the US House of Representatives, 112th Congress. "The Stanford Ponzi Scheme" hearing, May 13, 2011.

45 Anonymous, "The Londoner's Diary: Allen Stanford's Final Chukka," Evening Standard, Feb. 20, 2009.

46 Andy Hodgson, "Cricket's new mogul is thriving on adversity: Sir Allen Stanford and his family are used to making a profit when the going gets tough," Evening Standard, Oct. 28, 2008.

47 Churcher, "The English 'outside wife' who billionaire Stanford jilted at the altar...twice," Daily Mail, March 15, 2009.

48 Churcher and Parry, "Revealed: The secret of Sir Allen Stanford's three 'outside wives'," Daily Mail, March 1, 2009.

49 One wrote: "R Allen Stanford, the Texan billionaire who belongs in a Benny Hill sketch, is living proof money cannot buy class." Calvin, "Stanford's Proof That Money Can't Buy Class," Sunday Mirror Nov. 2, 2008.

50 The quote is from a State Department cable that was leaked and widely reported, for instance: "WikiLeaks cables: US suspected Allen Stanford long before ECB deal," by Gibson , The Guardian, Monday 20 December 2010, at guardian.co.uk, and "WikiLeaks: US diplomats warned about Stanford," in The Times of India, Dec. 22, 2010.

51 According to Davis.

52 Elfrink, "The Fall of a Titan," Miami New Times, April 09, 2009.

53 National Legal and Policy Center, "Request for an Investigation into Activities of Rep. Gregory Meeks," letter to the Congressional Committee on Standards of Official Conduct, March 19, 2010.

54 National Legal and Policy Center, "Request for an Investigation into Activities of Rep. Gregory Meeks," letter to the Congressional Committee on Standards of Official Conduct, March 19, 2010.

55 Smith, "Record show Rep. Gregory Meeks took six Caribbean trips with wife - on tab of con artist," Daily News, Dec.28, 2009.

56 Janvey v. Sjoblom.

57 "Second Amended Complaint" by the SEC, June 19, 2009.

58 Janvey v. Sjoblom.

59 Plea Agreement of James M. Davis, August 27, 2009. In this document, "outside attorney A" is obviously Sjoblom, as press reports recognized.

60US Securities and Exchange Commission Office of the Inspector General, "Investigation of the SEC's Response to Concerns Regarding Robert Allen Stanford's Alleged Ponzi Scheme," March 31, 2010; p. 131.

61 Ralph Janvey v. Democratic Senatorial Campaign Committee et. al., June 22, 2011.

62 "The Stanford Ponzi Scheme" hearing before the Subcommittee on Oversight and Investigations of the Committee on Financial Services of the US House of Representatives, 112th Congress, May 13, 2011.

63 "One On One With Stanford," interview on CNBC by Scott Cohn, April 20, 2009, at www.cnbc.com.

64 Roth, "A Washington Tale: As Feds Closed In, Stanford Boosted Efforts To Buy Influence," TPMMuckraker, January 5, 2010.

65 Robert Hoffman describes Stanford's insistence that employees wear the eagle pins. Sir Allen & Me: An Insider's Look at R. Allen Stanford and the Island of Antigua.

66 Davis' 2012 testimony.

67 Sallah and Barry, "As feds closed in, Allen Stanford scrambled to keep fraud secret, money flowing," Palm Beach Post, Dec. 6, 2009.

68 Stecklow, "Hard Sell Drove Stanford's Rise and Fall," Wall Street Journal, April 3, 2009.

69 Caribarena News. "Libya Rejects Stanford-Madoff Invite," 25 February 2011.

70 Foley, "Stanford's lawyers reveal his depression and alcohol abuse," The Independent, June 26, 2009.

71 Greenberg, "Crazy for Cricket," Forbes suppl. Forbes 400, October 6, 2008, p. 202.

72 Wyatt, "Former SEC Official Said to Be Subject of Criminal Inquiry," The New York Times, May 13, 2011.

73 "The Stanford Ponzi Scheme" hearing before the Subcommittee on Oversight and Investigations of the Committee on Financial Services of the US House of Representatives, 112th Congress, May 13, 2011.

74 Wilonsky "In Dallas Federal Court, Those Swindled by Allen Stanford Sue SEC For Failing to Stop Him," Dallas Observer, March 25 2011.

75 Baxter, "Andrews Kurth Sued for Malpractice Over Allen Stanford Work" The AMLaw Daily, April 14, 2011.

76 Harris, "Stanford Investors Accuse Lawyer, Law Firm of Aiding Fraud," Bloomberg News, August 29, 2009.

77 Paton "Who's Your Client?" In-House Counsel Spring 2010.

78 Protess, "SEC Official Demoted Despite Spotting Stanford," The New York Times, May 13, 2011.

79 "The Stanford Ponzi Scheme" hearing before the Subcommittee on Oversight and Investigations of the Committee on Financial Services of the US House of Representatives, 112th Congress, May 13, 2011.

80 United States v. Robert Allen Stanford, Motion to Reconsider and/or Reopen the Court's Detention Order, July 7, 2009.

81 The information comes from a video made of the investigation in the cell right after the incident.

82 Borland, "Tycoon Stanford Spits Up Blood In Court," Sky News Online, October 15, 2009.

83 United States v. Robert Allen Stanford, December 28, 2011, Order by Judge David Hittner.

84 Foley, "Stanford's lawyers reveal his depression and alcohol abuse," The Independent, June 26, 2009.

85 Stoffel, "You're Wrong about Madoff, and that Ignorance Will Hurt You," The Motley Fool, April 27, 2012.

86 US Securities and Exchange Commission v. Stanford International Bank et al., Receiver's Third Interim Report, Nov 11, 2011.

87 Janvey v. Democratic Senatorial Campaign Committee et. al. Order by David C. Godbey, June 22, 2011.

88 McElhatton, "Both parties scheme for Ponzi cash," The Washington Times, July 26, 2011.

Printed in Great Britain
by Amazon